Merry Christmas - 1993
To Dad,
With Love
From Junge & Gene

'Tis Me Again, B'y

'Tis Me Again, B'y

Andy MacDonald

BREAKWATER

Breakwater
100 Water Street
P.O. Box 2188
St. John's, Newfoundland
A1C 6E6

The Publisher gratefully acknowledges the financial
support of The Canada Council, which has helped make
this publication possible.

Canadian Cataloguing In Publication Data

MacDonald, Andy.

'Tis me again, b'y

ISBN 0-920911-42-0

I. Title.

PS8575.D66T57   1990   C813'.54   C90-097546-6
PR9199.3.M32T57   1990

Contents

Foreword

I dedicate this, my fourth book, to all those people who get such a kick out of my books, and especially to a great little lady at the Westford Nursing Home, Gerry MacKay, who enjoys my stories the way they should be enjoyed, and more than once has had to be rushed, laughing, to the toilet, in the middle of being read to. So here's hoping you, Gerry, and everyone else will spend many happy hours on the toilet while reading this newest book. Oh, and by the way, Gerry, quite a bit of interest has accrued on that dime you owe me for ice cream.

The following are some people I'd like to remember.

Ed Goodwin, a great guy, loved by everyone who knew him, and one of the funniest men I knew. He died a few years ago of cancer, but was comical to the end. Ed plays an important role in two or three of the stories in this book.

Chester Kay, a man in his early fifties from Baie Verte, N.B., who has a terrible memory. All he can remember are women, especially women by the name of Nancy.

Aunt Emma MacRae of Meadow Vista, in Oxford, N.S., a distant relative of a lady who threw me out of the doctor's office when I was trying to get warm. Aunt Emma is nothing like that relation of hers. She is a sweet, humorous lady and remarkably alert for her young age of 80 plus.

Stewart Gilbert Herald of Edwardsville, Cape Breton, who was always hired by my brother Billy to help him clean up our yard. I was always trying to escort 'Stooky' out of our yard by

7

pushing, shoving and fighting, so I could help Billy and get the money myself. 'Stooky' is also the one we gave all our gum to in *Tell Pa I'm Dead*. I think he still has some of it.

Harley Aloysius Lowe, a driver for Lane's Bread in Amherst, N.S., a little younger than me. (I believe he lies about his age.) He still thanks me for teaching him tube bending, when 'Canada Car' was thriving in the war years. I'll be glad when Little Harley (as we used to call him at work) retires, so he can take me fishing with him.

Harvey Cooper, a tall man from P.E.I. (about 5' 2"), a great salesman, who could almost sell you one shoe at a reduced price at his shoe store in the Amherst Mall.

Pete Fillmore and his wife Joyce, a most unforgettable couple, who are willing to help everyone they come in contact with. A very kind pair. If only they had a bigger garden.

Janet Irene Whatley, of North Sydney, Cape Breton, one of my greatest teenage fans, who is always so anxious for each one of my books to come out.

To all my brothers and sisters for all the hard times and humour we lived through over the years.

Much appreciation to my daughter Dianne. If it weren't for her long hours of editing, laughing and typing into the wee hours of the morning, I would not be on my fourth book and already planning a fifth. I'm also lucky that Dianne is so humorous and witty, joyous and beautiful; that's the type I love to work with. Furthermore, Dianne doesn't know I added this, so Dianne, I didn't forget you, did I?

David Andrew Copp, my oldest grandson. I blame every neck and shoulder pain I have today on him, because I carried him up there, like Tiny Tim, when he was a little kid, every place I went around the farm. I'd love try it today, but daren't take the chance. My weight is 135 and he, at 6' 4", tips the scales at 210. I'd be completely flattened.

Michael Stewart Copp, my youngest grandson, who must never forget that while it took his mom two pins to secure his diapers, on my babysitting nights, only one large safety pin did the trick. Michael always enjoyed those large diapers. That young boy needed plenty of space.

Many thanks to my wife, Rhoda, who has stuck with me through thick and thin. In the making of this book, I put all the blame on her each time I mislaid a page of the proofs. She'd try to sooth me over by bringing me some oatmeal cookies and tea. I could always eat that, even during an earthquake.

Carol Roberts, who sits ahead of me in church—when I go. She's very pretty and, with her new mauve hat and long, dark coat, could pass for the Archbishop of Canterbury. I belt out the hymns that I know right in her ear and then whisper the ones that are new to me.

The late Marley Hyde's wife, Gertie and family. Marley died a few years ago, but will be best remembered by me for the mouse wine we concocted when we were boys. The story of it, called "Eat, Drink and Be Mousey," is in my first book, *Bread and Molasses*.

Sid Walke and family of Coxheath. Sid was my seatmate in school. On the first day he fell asleep in my arms. Now fifty-three years later, he doesn't sleep at all. He's an insomniac. His eyes just won't close.

Veronica Leonard, who has been a great help to me in the promotion of all my books. She shoots from the hip and her articles are never stale. Port Elgin should be proud to have such a humorous newslady in their midst.

Dr. Marilyn Trenholm of Port Elgin, whom I've christened "The Laughing Doctor." She has kept me living this long with her pretty smile. She surprised me a while ago by telling me about my cholesteral. Why, for some years I had thought that cholesteral was something that crawled along the ground and belonged to the cockroach family.

And last, but not least, thank God that we got this manuscript finished; and many thanks to Nancy Brisbin for all her prayers.

Introduction

I'm still the same fellow as in the first three books, oddly enough, only I'm seventy-two now and holding. I just hope I'm around to see this book in the bookstores, what with all the falls, spills and smashes I've been taking lately. First I fell off the roof. Next, Rhoda placed a higher bureau in our bedroom than I was used to. I bent down in the night to put my slippers on to go to the bathroom, without turning on the light, and splatto, Rhoda found me under the bed in the morning.

The next incident I blame on my old setting hen. I felt sorry for her, sitting on her sixteen brown eggs in my big, cold barn. It was a frosty night in April when I decided to move her and her shelled brood to a warmer shed out back. Grabbing my clucking, pecking, pregnant hen under one arm and her unborn chillun in a basket in the other, I strode into the cold night air feeling quite pleased with myself that my old faithful brood hen would soon be rosy cozy on her eggs in a warm little room. Zap, I stepped on a patch of ice covered with a light dusting of snow, and hen and chicken in a basket flew in every direction, managing to fall KERPLOP! on the ice, with me falling on top of them. After that, all I had was a crushed and crippled hen and scrambled chicklets, as I floundered amidst feathers, shells and yolks.

This was probably the reason why the rooster decided to take out a contract on me the next week. I was once again coming out of the hen barn, having collected five eggs that had just been laid. From out of nowhere the rooster came flying at my head. I turned to make a grab for him, slipped on the same patch of ice, and down I went, KERBLAM! I managed to save three eggs from being broken, which I immediately pelted the rooster with. It was good to see him standing there with egg on his face.

Read about the first blind date I had with a dog bigger than a young foal, which kissed with frothy slobbers. Then there was the man I saved from a messy grave, having first I relieved him of his billfold. In "My First Will and Testament" you'll learn about what a time I had trying to get rid of my belongings; I know I'm going to have a lot of trouble trying to bribe Saint Peter with some loonies I want to get rid of.

I am still born in Cape Breton. My twin lives in California; Teedy in Virginia; Billy in Cape Breton; and me in New Brunswick. We're not quite as scared of Pa as we used to be.

So, if you don't get a good old-fashioned laugh out of this book, and my hens haven't done me in yet, phone me immediately; both you and I will go see a psychiatrist. And you can bring enough for the fee.

Anyway, relax and enjoy yourself and have a laugh. It's the best medicine. If you enjoyed the book, write me. If you didn't, write your Congressman.

Andy MacDonald
April 1990

Childhood

1

Childhood Memories

Murray and I were exactly one month old on 6 December 1917, the date of the Halifax Explosion. It didn't do us much damage, except to blow our diapers off. But that was okay, Ma was just getting ready to change us anyway.

My next recollection is of Ma putting a molasses cake away for company. We'd had no company for days and she'd forgotten about it. It was all dry and hard by the time she put it in front of us, and we turned up our noses at it. Then all she did was make a frosting for it, and before the frosting was set, the cake was gone.

At odd times, a visitor to our house would give each of us brothers a nickel. We had to sit for hours, staring up into his eyes like hungry dogs, until he produced our nickels. Then we'd lessen our stares until his next visit. But with those nickels, we talked our sisters, who were going uptown for the evening, into bringing us back ice cream cones. Of course, we would be in bed asleep before they got home, and we would feel them poking us, saying, "Here's your ice cream." Eyes closed, we'd sit up, then reach out, trying to enjoy what tasted like a delicious piece of sweetened paper, as the cones were now small balls. (It was June and everything had melted.) We didn't really get our money's worth in the summer, but it never stopped us asking our sisters to bring us ice cream cones home again.

A neighbour not far from us had a tremendous garden that yielded anything he planted; an abundance of vegetables for him and his wife. Adjoining his garden was a field almost a mile long which housed one cow. When his garden began yielding its crops, the man would toss vines of string beans,

15

peas and small carrots to the cow. Billy, Murray, Teedy and I were always waiting for that throw. We'd wait until the man went back to his house. Bravely we would shoo the cow away and pick through the garden produce, always succeed- ing in getting a mess of vegetables for our supper. How happy Ma would be when she saw us coming with an armful of veggies, with the cow staring at us as if to say, "That was supposed to be for my supper."

We loved candy, and at Halloween we didn't have to worry about candies being spiked with things as you do today. There was never much money spent on masks, but don't think I'm going to say we didn't need them, because we were just as pretty as you all are today. We made our own halloween suits. We were blessed with five sisters and a mother, so it wasn't hard for us to get a dress, pyjamas or a skirt to dress in for the evening. We had painted pasteboard masks, but why they didn't make larger eye and mouth holes, I don't know! The masks were okay if you had eyes the size of a bird and a mole mouth. Almost totally blind, and getting no air through the mouth or the nostrils, it was torture if you had to walk far. Your breathing would dampen the mouth, your tongue would poke through, and soon you'd be sucking paint off the mask.

One Halloween my older sister, Anne, helped my brother Billy all afternoon, getting him ready for a party; homemade face, wig, clothes. A few hours after she had finished with him, the two came face to face. Anne, on meeting this stranger so abruptly, was terrified and tore Billy's false face to shreds, having taken hours to assemble him.

Elastic was no good to keep the face on with, because by the end of the night the elastic had stretched so badly you'd have to have a head the size of a moose to hold the false face on. The mask always had a back exit as well as a front, or we would have smothered and would have had to carry nitro-glycerine pills on us, for the heart. We learned never to jump even one strand of barbed wire with our sisters' dresses on; Teedy, the youngest, tried it once, and in seconds was almost nude.

No one ever gave us money. We mostly got apples, some so hard we'd have to make three attempts to start the first bite. Candies were a novelty, but there were a few houses that gave you a penny candy. One old fellow who lived alone wasn't a bit scroogy at treating, but we never liked his treat. He'd get you to cup your hands and then he'd pour some corn flakes in it.

We played some pranks, but nothing in comparison to what they do today. One of our henchmen friends didn't like a certain treat, so he let out twenty-five of the man's pigs. What a snorting time that was, with the pigs stampeding right through the centre of town. Another buddy was chased by the police for some misdemeanour, and he was doing all right until his sister's drawers broke loose, his legs locked and he fell to the ground, the same as having been caught in a dragnet.

There were no laws against fire crackers, sparklers or sky rockets then, so we were shooting them off everywhere.

Even though we never got much candy for Halloween, here are a few kinds of candies that were sold in our day.

Hunk a Dory—sugar coated candy about eight inches long.

Ladies Choice—the very sweet stuff in the centre would drive a quiet bad tooth insane if it ever touched it.

Bucket Full of Boston Beans—the old lady would dip a small paper tub into these candies.

Honeymoons—two for a cent, very tasty.

Black Balls—three for a cent, took a week to suck one through to the end to get the kernel.

Caramels—four for one cent (all coloured paper).

Piece of Marshmallow—shaped like a small hut. Ripping through this white substance, you came to what you were looking for, a little black man made of licorice. It wasn't long before we ate hut and black man.

Red and green Square Suckers—tasty and lasting, with a true flavour, not like the imitations you get today.

Spearmint, Juicy Fruit and Doublemint Gum—one penny each stick.

Piccaninny Gum—when you opened your stick of Piccaninny gum, if it was black, that meant you had won a full package. We even made a racket out of this. We'd keep the black stick of gum and show it to the old lady again and again to get more free packs, until she caught on to us and took the black stick each time we found one.

Jelly Beans—small containers, same as the Boston Beans.

Licorice Tobacco—this had a small tin insignia on the tobacco, just like the real stuff.

Ice Cream Cones—they were filled with a maple and marshmallow concoction.

Coconut Bon Bons—one for one cent. Were they tasty! And browned at the top, quite large to put in your mouth all at one time. I just loved them and one day, seeing an unwanted friend coming towards my small bag of candy, which contained two bon bons, I stuffed the two in my mouth at once and could do nothing but nod for minutes, until I could navigate the upper and lower teeth and tunnel a hole through.

Jerusalem—a rainbow-coloured candy, very sticky, which would last a long time. About two inches long and half an inch thick.

Fluffy Marshmallow—about five inches long, loaded with burnt coconut. What a buy for a cent.

Candy Cigarettes—a box of five was one cent.

Peppermints—four for one cent.

Kisses—three for one cent.

Queen's Own Lunch—good, square-shaped chocolate, full of coconut.

Jaw Breakers—one for a cent. Red, orange and lemon, big as a big, open mouth. Sugar coated. Lasted forever and a day. I'm still sucking one.

Hard Hats—two for a cent, a beautiful tasting, sticky candy, a toffee taste.

Bachelor Buttons or Paper Buttons—white buttons on a piece of paper. Never liked the taste, kind of a powdery flavour like doctors pills.

Licorice Pipes, Cigars, Whistles and Whips—all great to start teeth aching.

During the first twelve years of my childhood, we had only one lamp. Eight or ten of us would gather around a large table, studying lessons, with the shadow of a big head strewn across our readers. When someone had to go into another room, he would say in a mumble, "Taking this lamp for a minute." It was then we meditated in darkness— a great blessing instead of studying.

When a rap came on our door, it was just an "Excuse me" as one of us reached for the lamp, even if one brother was trying to extract a pebble from another brother's eye and had his lower lid pulled down almost to his navel, just ready to seize the foreign object. The knock took priority, so the brother would have to release the lid.

If it was the teacher for one of us, it wasn't hard to get rid of her. We would load up with air, screw our mouths over to one side and blow down into the lamp flue. The light would go out and although it might be only seven o'clock on a winter's night, we'd tell her everyone was in bed.

One dark night in winter, a rap came on the door. I was closest to the lamp, so I seized it and ran to open the door. The party had a horse and sled. They must have figured no one was home because as I opened the door, he was on his way to the sled. Still carrying the lamp, I ran toward the sled as it was turning. Don't think that sock feet on ice patches aren't slippery! I spun for seconds and then took a staggering drop in front of the sleigh, trying to hold on to the lamp. The base of the lamp came out okay, but the lamp flue was in pieces.

Then came the excuse for the broken flue. "The man in the sled was drinking and threw a glove at the lampshade. He took off before I knew who he was." By then, Pa and everyone else had had enough meditation for the day and we all went to bed for a twelve-hour rest.

Born and brought up on cliffs that dropped to the Atlantic, the shores were our playground in summer. The whole town dumped their refuse over the cliffs. Not just garbage, but dead animals— horses, cows, pigs, dogs— everything that died, except humans. Most times the carcasses, which ended up close to the cliff, would stay there for months and rot in the heat.

On a hot day on our way to search the dump, through hundreds of blowflies, blackflies and mosquitos, we saw the decomposed body of a horse which had been picked to pieces so much you couldn't tell its gender. After viewing the remains, the custom was to step up to the creature's head and spit, at the same time saying, "No fever in our house." Still suffering through all the flies and the odour, if your spit missed the head, you were soon reminded by someone in the bunch. Then you'd struggle, waving away flies and holding your nose, and on your second trip you made sure you struck it square on the head.

Contented, you'd come back to your friend as though you had a complete doctor's certificate that you would never contract any disease whatsoever. You didn't have to remind him that he had to go through the same ritual, using the same sentence, "No fever in our house," if he hit the head.

Sometimes, when the smell was really rank, you'd have to make four or five trips before you would strike the head. Murray, my twin, was stricken with scarlet fever during one hot summer; we always told Ma that Murray missed the horse's head, because there was hardly any flesh left on it.

I remember when I was first learning to swim, we practised in water that the miners washed in. It drained out into a big pool next to the Atlantic. No matter how cold the Atlantic or the air temperature was, the Gut was almost at a boiling point. There was a continuous flow, and on cool days a bunch of us would run in right up to our necks. We were frolicking around in about 600 miners' bath water.

One day in particular, my buddy, Marley, invited two nice looking girls to the water. Beforehand, Marley said, "Let's pretend to them that we can swim. I told them you and I usually swim in the ocean."

The bottom of the Gut felt like you were standing in a foot of molasses. It had something to do with the different soaps the miners used. And there were all different levels. The girls couldn't get over the temperature of the water. Marley and I stuck our chests out and took all the credit for it. The girl that I loved, and would have married right in the water, hollered, "Andy, let's see you do the dog paddle." Marley and his girlfriend were all smiles, waiting for me to perform.

Down I got on all fours like a clumsy cow and tried to give them the impression I was swimming as I crawled along the bottom, grabbing handfuls of thick, gooey paste. Letting them believe I was paddling gracefully through the warm water, without warning I crawled right into a deep hole and went well over my head. I'm sure I was there covered over with water for hours, brains and lungs full of dirty miners' water; I know I breathed in many times under there. I can't say what happened next, except that God gave me a shove up, or I would have been there yet.

Up I came and looked around. Not one soul was watching me. They were yards and yards away. Every part of my body looked like someone had thrown a bucket of slime on me. So I was thankful they weren't looking at me. They weren't the least bit concerned about me; and here, seconds before, underwater, I was being introduced to people who had died five years before. Why, if my girlfriend had been watching from start to finish, she would have told everyone about the half-hour I spent underneath the warm water. How proud she would have been, boasting of me to non-swimmers, not knowing that someplace underneath that warm, dirty water I had been singing "Abide With Me" with a choir of angels all clad in bikinis.

2

Treasures Galore

When we were kids, we didn't leave out anyone or anything we could initiate into our adventures, except Pa. And having read about the famous Captain Kidd, we thought we would incorporate his tactics into our lives for a while.

One evening, about twenty-five of us kids held a very stinging conversation and decided to go through all the qualms of a real treasure hide. Naturally, by majority, brother Bill was selected as Kidd, but not too heartily by his three brothers. Although we went along with their choice, we knew in our hearts that the others had made their first big mistake. It was like putting the fox in charge of the hens. We should have vetoed his selection because we knew him much better than they did. We didn't have very much to ourselves at home, but the little we did have was always forfeited to Billy, with some promise of good he made to us, but never followed through on.

Everybody in the gang was supposed to bring something shiny, not too large, but of some value; and if by chance you could get more, all the better for the rest of us magpies, especially Bill.

Maps were quickly drawn up, pencilling in all the routes over the shores, through the town and right to the burying site not far from our house. Next, the container which held the valuables, a two- by three-foot metal box, was secretly taken to Bill, down through the field in front of our house, next to the cliffs. Valuables included watch chains, old coins, pocket watches, gold rings and glasses, all beautiful to look at and fondle. When we saw all the valuables that the gang had snatched from their parents, it wasn't just Billy, the dictator, whose eyes lit up. I remember there was a gold ring with a lion's face on it, and my, how I pictured my hand and the position I would hold it in to show the ring off to Renee, the girl in school I had a secret crush on. When Bill was putting it in the box with the rest, I almost reached in and said, "I've got to have this ring now." Each valuable was set carefully in the box and the lid gently closed. They were to rest undisturbed under three feet of earth until digging time.

Sitting around the hole on our honkers, in Indian fashion, the twenty-five of us were watching our very crooked Captain Kidd gently holding the box of goodies. It was quite heavy now, with all the donations in it. We three brothers were a little surprised that Billy hadn't taken the box right home with him then and emptied it before the crowd dispersed; but acting like an honest patriarch, he stayed with the crowd, for now.

Then in a manner of great drama, Billy gave the confidential whisper, like Marcos of the Philippines, that he'd take care of everyone's interests till death do them part. With many exaggerated hand motions similar to Ed Norton on the "Honeymooners," a map was presented to each person. I can still see Teedy, the youngest in the bunch, bowing and scraping and bowing and bowing, like a little Japanese premier. Teedy even looked Oriental, with his round little face.

Once this was done, we all lowered the box to its final resting place with much pomp and ceremony, hand shaking and bowing to each other like we had just signed the Declaration of Independence. The agreement was that the treasure chest would be dug up and opened a year from the burying time.

For a few days, the mother and father of every kid who belonged to the organization was in a dilemma, searching for things that were missing from their home. Earlier, at the meeting, this dilemma had been anticipated by the pirates. The members were to go along with their parents, searching for the objects, even shedding tears about their loss, much the same as Billy did in my first book, *Bread and Molasses,* when, side by side with Pa, he helped him look for his missing white sweater, which Billy had died red and just happened to be wearing at that very moment. Everything worked out fine. Helping their parents look for their cherished objects only lasted a few days. Then everything blew over and all was forgotten, giving the clan full ownership of the treasure.

Headquarters for our meetings was an old barn. We were all garbed in bandanas and eye patches and were toying with the idea of cutting off someone's leg, preferably Pa's, so we could have a Pegleg Pete in our midst. Probably Pa wouldn't even have minded once we showed him all the treasure we had and if we had gotten him a parrot to wear on his wrist.

Bill, the head man and instigator of the scheme, was busy outlining our maps on larger pieces of paper, the kind we did our school exams on— foolscap. He used a red pencil, which made them look really legal. But the most authentic thing we had was some hard red wax stuck to the signature of evil Billy. The wax stick belonged to Pa, we lifted it from his bookcase. To use it, you lit it with a match, then while it was hot you could seal an envelope with it. I think Pa kept it in case he ever became President of the U.S.A. He would have used it at his inauguration. It was no good for anything else. We even tried to chew it, but it was as hard as steel and broke our teeth. It only softened when you lit it.

So Captain Kidd and his kids set out to follow the arrows on the map. This was to satisfy ourselves that the route would take us to the same spot we started from, kind of like proving the earth was round by coming back to the same spot again on the path. A path, I might add, that would be much trodden by Billy.

Happy smiles were evident as the kids folded their maps, placed them inside their shirts and took them home. They were to be hidden until a year later, when a specific day would be announced for the unveiling of the treasure.

Then one evening about a week later, feeling the time was ripe, and with all the other pirates safe in their homes, Captain Billy the Kidd, with his gestapo help, namely Murray, Teedy and me, came up with an idea. Dusk made it more exciting to unravel our daring plan. We would remove the treasure box, pick the best of the loot, then lower it and try to abide by the rest of the rules until a year from then, if we could.

Bill's prize was to be an old antique watch. He told us this at the first shovelful. Mine was the lion ring. Teedy's was some chains and Murray's, coins. That night we hardly slept, with pirate dreams floating through our minds as we fondled our stolen treasures. Billy rigged up an old kerosene lamp, which we kept burning behind closed doors, surveying every part of our grabbed loot. My fingers were tired and sore from trying on the ring all night, from one hand to the other and from finger to finger, then studying the angle that would be best for Renee to absorb my handsomeness. Murray was jingling coins as if he was in the circus, running one of their crooked wheels. And Teedy, with his chains, looked much the same as Mr. T does today.

Billy drilled it into our heads not to carry or wear our risen treasures anywhere in case we ran into the pirate who had seized it from his parents in the first place.

Everything was hunky-dory for awhile. Then caution blew away. Billy, the head crook, carelessly made a big mistake. He had noticed that the treasure watch with the gold chain on it made his old blue pants look really dressy; and that by hanging the chain loosely out through the belt loops, it gave him the look of a Senator. Billy proudly, swankily and thoughtlessly wore this watch to a show one day, to show off to his girlfriend; next day she told everyone in school about it. This started quite a commotion amongst the pirates at school and an urgent meeting was called, with all the members wanting their booty back.

Hardly did the meeting end when Billy and his three accomplices made a beeline for the treasure mound to open the ground again. It was a very dark night as we ran along the top of the cliffs to where the buried treasure lay. We dug feverishly in the earth where we had so recently reinterred the treasure, so we could return the borrowed objects. Mud flying everywhere in the darkness, the shovel at last found its way through the mud. Four pairs of hands reached down to retrieve the treasure, when a ghastly cry of "Yagggggg" came from our lips. As we put our hands in the hole, all we could feel was fur. Murray had grabbed a paw, Teedy a tail, and I had a hold of a dog's nose. Someone had stolen the treasure and replaced it with a dead dog.

At that moment, the moon came out and illuminated the field. There was another mound about twenty feet along the path. That was our treasure mound. Digging and digging, we found the box and flipped open the lid.

Murray, Teedy and I put our grab back. I didn't take it too badly because Renee had been in the hospital with appendicitis the whole time I was sporting the ring. But Billy still sported the watch. Lowering the box for the third time made us feel much better, because the next night it would be lifted out again by all the treasure holders, and we'd be found guiltless, all except Bill. And though he would rather have absconded to the West Indies on his pirate ship, Billy the Kidd had no alternative but to be at the grave opening the next evening. Billy didn't want to give up his watch, because there were very few movie stars who got as much publicity as he did. At times signing autographs, he looked rich and no one could deny it. He even forced Teedy, Murray and me to accept his autograph.

Nothing was said as the box was dug up and placed on the ground. Each kid grabbed all his mum's and dad's possessions. But it took a solid day of arguing before Billy would give back the watch that was dressing him up to be something he wasn't. Sid, the kid who finally got his father's watch back, got it back only because he threatened to hire a Philadelphia lawyer. Sid then took the watch home, put it in a place where his dad wouldn't think of looking, edged him up to the secret place and watched the surprised look on his father's face as he grasped the hand-me-down watch given him by his grandfather.

Had Captain Kidd the traitors in his outfit we had, it would be stupid to spend money searching for his loot today. It wouldn't be there. How do we know that he didn't have our same grabbing personality; as soon as it was buried, the Kidd himself, greedy for some of the precious gems he saw being lowered into the ground, a short time later came back and helped himself as we had done.

And where were the maps Kidd was supposed to have passed out? At least Billy was kind enough to give us each a detailed map to the very spot where he got tangled up in the love of a little gold watch and chain that matched his attire and sent his batting average to a tremendous high with the opposite sex. No wonder he was so reluctant to give it up. But he almost had to, because Sid said fitting punishment for such a dastardly deed was to bury Billy standing up in the sand at the edge of the beach, making sure the sand came right up to his neck, and leave him there all day in the hot sun until the tide came in. And while Billy would have drowned, I think he would have held his arm up until the last and saved that precious watch. As it was, to tell the time, Billy ended up with a cheap Westclox watch with a braided cod line for a chain, and I sort of slowed down the hand twirling I had been getting accustomed to.

3

The Night Billy Slept With a Pig

One spring, Pa decided to buy a sow pig and have her bred. We all vowed to do everything to help the piglets grow, short of giving them our breakfast porridge. Pa wasn't long erecting a not-too-elaborate-looking pig box. In a half-hour, he had muzzled the sow and was shoving her toward the box on an old truck he had borrowed from a friend. With a half-hitch around her snout, Pa was hauling on the small rope like the Volga boatman and grunting more than the pig.

To get her up the ramp, we four brothers were shoving with all our might on her hind hams, like we were trying to push the Hindenburg. If she had let go, all four of us would have flown out through the cab of the truck like we were shot from a rifle. Figuring we were trying to seduce her into a torture chamber, and as if she had air brakes on all fours, the pig came to a complete halt in the centre of the ramp and smiled in pig fashion, as if to say, "There, what do you think of that, smartiepants?"

Pa, tugging furiously, gave a command from the entrance to twist her tail. We wasted time wondering which one of us had the nerve to do it because, who knows, the tail might have wrapped around our necks like a boa constrictor and strangled us, or it may have had poison venom in the tip.

It was Teedy's little fat hand that reached the pig's tail first. He yanked it really hard. But the only pigtails he'd ever pulled were on girls, and they didn't grunt and snort afterward. Teedy, white as paper, didn't lessened his yank and almost tore the tail out of its moorings.

Halfway up the ramp, I gave the pig a quick smack with the stick I carried. The sow threw its full weight against the sideboard we had just made and off the ramp she fell, taking three of the boards with her. Jumping down, I covered her head with my coat until I got help. Tying her legs and putting a half-nelson around her snout so she could barely snort, we held her motionless on the ground. We then lifted the pig's dead weight onto the top of the ramp and untied her.

The sow took a sudden short plunge forward, then applied her brakes again to all four of her unpickled pigs' feet. Another screech from Pa demanded more tail twisting. It was hard to tell who was making the most noise, Pa or the pig. Teedy gave the tail another mighty wrench, and Pa stepped aside just in time or there would have been two in the pig box. Then which one of us would have been brave enough to twist Pa's tail to get him out of there?

In minutes, the pig was strutting along the pig box, looking at us as if to say, "I took quite a tumble back there, didn't I, boys? Do any of you know anything about farming or agriculture?"

The date of the piglets arrival was circled on the calendar half-an-hour after the sow left her husband's bedside. Two days before the blessed event, Marie, the sow, in her prettiest and piggiest maternity smock, was putting on the last acts of pregnancy, wanting oodles of dill pickles and ice cream mixed with mud, and all of us were getting heartburn. Ms. Piggy wouldn't sit, stand, drink warm milk or yodel. Billy was reading Dr. Spock; I was studying Lamaze delivery; and Murray was knitting booties. Teedy was having labour pains, but we didn't dare tell Pa, in case he took him to the vet.

Soon Mrs. Sow came forth with twelve chunks of red, uncooked pork. Pa was still working, so we took in every angle of the delivery. We weren't very brave around Piggly Wiggly Marie now, because she was making some new grunts we had never heard before, which seemed to mean, "If you set one foot toward my little piggies, I'll bite off your face, you nose bags."

Fact is, we had been deathly scared of the sow before she had her brood. Pa used to walk right into the pen with the pig, but we never even opened the door for fear she'd burst out like a charging rhinoceros and swallow us whole. Instead, we would reach over the pen very carefully to feed her so as not to ruffle her bristles.

One day Teedy, engrossed in all the little piggies zipping around, climbed up the rough boards of the pen and took a somersault into the middle of the pig family. In the midst of grunts and squeals, mostly Teedy's, and before they could have him for their supper, we threw an eight-foot board into the pen and he ran up it like a kitten, dripping in sludge.

A few days after the pigs' birth, we heard Pa tell a neighbour that the little pigs would grow better and produce more meat if they were castrated. That word was a little large to fit into our vocabulary. Billy told us it meant they'd have their tails bobbed. We didn't asked Pa what it meant, in case he suggested that we have it done to us so that we'd grow better and produce more meat.

One night when Pa arrived from the mine, he was accompanied by the vet, who put each one of the pigs asleep, did his dirty deed, and then told Pa that when the little pigs came to, probably in less than an hour, they were going to be awfully hungry and very thirsty, because they would be fevered. He said to be prepared to give them lots of warm milk and water with a swish of feed, and then put them back with their mother.

For the first three hours the shed was noiseless, as twelve red-faced snouts looked peacefully dead. Whatever anaesthetic the vet had administered to them, we wished we could have used to keep Pa asleep.

While we were waiting, we heated water in a big soup pot, poured it into smaller pots for each pig and added a dash of milk. Finally, zero hour arrived, with the four of us and Pa holding onto the pots and our hats. A welcome yawn from a big mouth was the first sign. That was Pa. This set off a chain reaction. Nine piglets again came into the world, but with a lot more ferocity than when we were midwives.

Springing up by using their back muscles, they leaped a foot off the floor, like they were on a trampoline. Not one to be outdone, so did Billy. He chased them all around the place until finally their round, cheese-like snouts found the warm milk. Sloshing, gulping, pushing, burping and tail twirling, a couple had their fill and were puffed up like balloons. But nobody could move fast enough to please the other hungry oinks, or Pa. As fast as Pa filled the pots, they gobbled it down and stole the next fellow's share when it took a breather, like brother Murray often did when we were piglets.

Another three gallons of water with milk was warmed and delivered to Pa to try to satisfy red hot stomachs. And we thought Murray could eat a lot! Nine pigs were nestled back with their momma, looking playful. We even begrudged the pigs the milk. We never got the treatment they were getting. They would leap and run for a bit, then stand perfectly still, like they were posing for their mother so they could tell her, "Now take a good long look at us and tell us if they messed with our hind parts. Whatever they did, it's interfered with our walking."

It was now eight-thirty at night. Still three more pigs to go. The pigs that were left looked like they weren't going to make it like the rest, and neither did we. Their pink snouts looked like chewed-up bubble gum, and their small curly tails were nearly straight, and so were ours. Under finely plucked eyebrows, eyelashes were locked together. We couldn't see a pulse jumping anywhere on their bodies. And our pulses weren't too active either, until we'd receive another command from Pa.

Nine o'clock, then ten— no movement. Pa suggested we carry them into the house and wait for their gluttonish awakening. Pa went off to bed. We four dwindled to two. At twelve, Billy and I volunteered to keep the vigil and light a candle. Teedy and Murray staggered upstairs.

One o'clock, two o'clock. Why, the vet had almost guaranteed that they wouldn't be under more than an hour. We definitely had to get some of his stuff to put Pa out like a light on weekends. At three o'clock they were still out. Billy and I were exhausted. Pa's orders were to stay with the pigs through earthquakes, typhoons or attacks of gout. But what if the last pigs were dead? Were we to accompany them to the grave? Should we be buried alive with them? Billy had given the pigs the last rites, and now he and I were watching every part of them, waiting for a twitch, the only two ever to attend a pig's wake.

If Murray and Teedy hadn't spread their bodies so much across the bed that slept four, we could have taken the pigs to bed with us. I'm sure the pigs would have awakened after all the pokes from eight flying feet, not to mention the smell of them. Teedy's feet smelled worse than the pigpen.

The pigs were still in the same position on the floor, with one open ear that had stood erect since they'd been put asleep. I told Billy that if I were a pig and someone poured cold water in my ear, I would squirm, even if I was dead. I ran to the sink and filled up a cup. Holding the water about six inches from a hairy open ear, I funnelled it in. The water just stayed there like in a paper cup. There was no sign of life in any hock. The ear must have been clogged. We should have had the pigs' ears syringed before the operation.

Then Billy decided he'd go to sleep on a small cot in the kitchen where the pigs were. We blocked off the openings to the pantry, the porch and the small cupboard where we kept the flour, as if preparing for a Martian invasion. I slept on three chairs in the adjoining room, well barricaded against Rip Van Winkle's entry, if he ever woke up.

It seemed I had been sleeping for weeks when I heard a commotion out where Billy was sleeping— a ripping sound, then long grunts accompanied by a racing spree and squeals of delight which weren't coming from Billy. It was minutes before I knew who or where I was— perhaps Clark Gable in a brothel— only to hear more tearing. Peeking into the kitchen where Billy still lay dreaming, the baby wild boars had torn off all the wallpaper on the wall next to Billy's cot and were just starting to rip into his feet, his elbows and his ears.

I ran in with a pot of drink just as one was trying to bite off a few of Billy's toes, as if he were snapping off candy canes. Steering his round snout to the fluid that would cool his stomach and save Billy's limbs, the pig gave one awful grunt and an enraged squeal, the likes of which we'd often heard out of Pa. He couldn't get the liquid into him fast enough. He should have sucked it up through his nose holes, like two giant straws, but you try telling that to a savage pig without getting your face chewed off.

Once the pig had received his overdose of water and milk, he lay down on his side, and his saucy little blue eyes with their silky grey lashes looked at Billy and me with a "Who are you? Why am I here? Where's the rest of the gang? And how about those Maple Leafs?" expression.

It was harder to wake Billy than it was to wake the pigs. I did everything but put water in his ear; I often wondered if I hadn't come to his rescue, how much of Billy the pigs would have eaten. At last he came to, and with the two of us working as a team we got them all fed, then made our way out to the mother with a pig under each arm. We threw them in at her and they bounced off her buttocks like silly putty.

It was good to go to bed knowing that while we slept we weren't going to be attacked by small pigs charging us like a mad bull.

Billy and I had just snuggled down into bed and dropped quickly off to sleep when the whole household was awakened by Teedy, having what could only have been called a pig fit, screeching and hollering at the top of his loud lungs, "The pigs are coming up the stairs!" With what Billy and I had just lived through, they may have been. Still half asleep, I grabbed an old baseball bat that was under the bed and Billy grabbed the pot. Luckily it was empty. We stumbled into the hallway to meet Pa with his eyes half closed, holding a crowbar, and Murray, both eyes closed, grasping a rubber boot in each hand. With our boots, crowbar, bat and pot, we were going to bash those evil pigs to within an inch of their lives. We heard Teedy again, from inside the bedroom, "They're coming up the stairs!" We then began to wonder how Teedy knew the pigs were coming up the stairs if he was still in the bed. He would have to be a pig psychic. It didn't take us too long to get Teedy back into his right mind again; off we all drifted to sleep, to continue our full nap.

It couldn't have been more than a half an hour later when it happened all over again, with Teedy screaming in delirium, "Here come the pigs! Here they come!" Up we all jumped once more in our different styles of night attire, with Pa in his long johns standing over our bed as Teedy told us about how the mother pig had reached under the covers while he was sleeping and sniffed and snorted at his leg.

Pa tried to coax Teedy to sleep the rest of the night with him, but he wanted to stay with his brothers. So Pa said, "Now you close your eyes and dream about eating ice cream and forget about those old pigs." Then Pa whispered to us we were never to keep Teedy up this late again with something of this nature, because it stayed in his mind too long, probably because he was the youngest.

So off we went to sleep again, everyone dreaming peacefully about grass skirts in Hawaii and the Philippines when suddenly Pa rushed into our bedroom, pulled on the light chains and had his posse around him in minutes. It was Pa who had snapped this time. He said he had heard a snorting and squealing sound downstairs and wondered if we had closed the gate to the pen. I told Pa that even of we had forgotten to close the gate, none of the piglets or the mother had the key to our house, so it couldn't possibly have been them. It was then that Pa said, "We'll be buying our pork in barrels after this. It's much easier to get some sleep."

Next morning, after our pig-filled night, we stumbled downstairs and ate our porridge respectfully and not like a pig except, of course, for Murray. Meanwhile, all these years Bill has tried to keep it a secret from his wife that he once slept with a pig. Not exactly the kind of thing you'd like to get around, especially for the pig. And when Billy buys bacon, pork chops or ham, he's still embarrassed to bring it home, even though his wife doesn't smell a rat. I know I'll never tell. But, can pigs talk?

4

The Telephone Operator
Should Have Bought Us A Clock

One cold night when it was my turn to put Pa off to work in the mine the next morning at five o'clock, I knew I had to set the alarm for four o'clock so I would have time to make his lunch, start the fire and get his breakfast. Looking disgustedly at the clock, I reached for it and slipped my finger through the ring at the top, like a yo-yo; the clock fell heavily to the floor like a boulder.

Miraculously, it ticked relentlessly on, and the body didn't even break. But the alarm wouldn't ring. It was like a person who could whisper, but not holler. It had laryngitis.

Pa had bought it a few months before, so telling him about the accident would be like telling him I'd murdered his mother. From then on, it kept three heads going all night so the victim whose turn it was to put Pa off wouldn't oversleep. What a siege we put in. We all worried about one another and carried baggy sacks under our eyes to prove it.

Then we got an idea. Before we went to bed each night, we would whisper to the telephone operator, as if we were divulging government secrets to the enemy, that our clock was broken and that we were scared to tell Pa. In fact, I don't think the operator was too brave about Pa, though all she knew was his voice. We asked her to give us a very weak ring at four a.m. (Heck, Pa was paying them $2.40 a month. That was money, man.) She agreed, so from then on, as if waiting in dread for an air raid, each night we twisted and turned, waiting to hear the phone. Then a brother, as soon as he was awakened by the jingle of the phone, would almost rupture you with a kick, saying, "It's the operator." Then we'd fly softly down the stairs and, still in third gear, answer with a timid "Thank you" so Pa wouldn't hear. Then back upstairs like quiet, woolly-footed mice, into our pants and right back down again into the kitchen to fill Pa's can and make his porridge. I believe the operator suffered all night like the rest of us, until she got Pa's call off her chest at four every morning, because you could hear her heave a tired sigh.

One day, Murray, hearing the faint tinkle of the phone at four o'clock, rushed out of our bedroom and fell halfway down the stairs. When it rang the second time, he picked up the receiver and said, "I fell. Thanks."

If we had known for sure Pa was in bed for the night, we could have set up a small cot downstairs beside the phone. But you never knew when Pa was going to get up for a glass of water or one last good rage at us. If he'd seen the bed, he'd have thought we were taking in boarders and making money to buy cigarettes on the side. If Pa had only known that I was thinking of boarding him close to the mine, or even in it, and paying for his rent with the money I made picking cranberries at three cents a pound.

One morning when it was Murray's turn to get up with Pa, we were so tired that we all overslept. We didn't hear a thing. Since we had the coldest room in the house, Pa fell for Murray's oversleeping excuse; he told Pa the clock froze. It seemed logical to Pa, once he had tested the temperature in our room. They could have kept newly slaughtered beef there without danger of spoiling, up until July.

After fooling around with Big Ben proudly ticking off the time in seconds like a bomb ready to explode, Pa tried the alarm and said, "One of you fellows take this clock back to the co-operative store tomorrow and get them to alarm it. Why, it's a new clock!"

Of course, the manager couldn't get it to ring either, so he opened up a new box and picked out one identical to ours. This one gave off a wondrous alarm, the sound we used to hate in the early mornings. But now it was like the "Sound of Music" minus Julie Andrews. We thought we'd at least get more sleep.

At home, we placed the clock on its special shelf. As soon as Pa wasn't around, we contacted the operator and told her quite proudly, but in a muffled whisper like James Bond, that she didn't have to call us any more because we'd gotten a new clock. Through my sneaky whisper, I heard her reply, "Well, it's about time you got one." And I wasn't the least bit insulted.

We were always pretty chummy with the operator. We thought we owned her, that she lived in the wall of our house. Hardly an hour passed without one of us asking her to look up someone's number. It didn't even put us out any when the operator, butting into our conversation with someone, would say, "Why don't you fellows hang up for a while. You're always on the phone!" A tremendous smile would spread across our faces when Teedy would relate this order from the operator, as though she'd just complimented us and said, "I love you four children. You're sweet."

She must have put together a good picture of what our family was like, especially when we were in deep conversation with a girl and Pa showed up. No goodbye or kisses. Just the fast click of the receiver. The operator had never met Pa, but I'm sure she could have written a book about him.

We asked her so many times what time it was that she finally said, "Why don't you look at your own clock?" It sort of stunned us for a minute, her sauciness, but it wore off in seconds after the fire whistle blew. Then we phoned her and asked her where the fire was before she had a chance to find out herself.

The first time Teedy got up to put Pa off to work, he made an early call to the operator with the crucial question, which was whispered quite loudly as he was too short for the phone, "How much salt should I put in Pa's porridge?" It's a wonder we didn't drive her crazy. I think we had her mesmerized.

No matter what good care we took of anything, or how much we worried about it, especially the clock, the faster the accidents happened. A few months after the new clock arrived, it was getting used to its new perch close to the hooks where our coats hung. It wasn't quite as shy with us as at first, when it used to blush a lot and hide behind a coat when you looked at it.

We were all feeling happy at the smooth way things were going. Even the clock looked full of fun, as if it wanted to jump off the shelf onto the floor and come play with us, but we never coaxed it. We were especially happy because Pa wasn't home. Happiness in Pa's absence often reached great heights, equivalent to being told you were to receive a large box of chocolates every day of your life until you burst.

Billy pranced into the kitchen, removed his winter cap and told us he has just learned how to ring hooks with it from a distance of fifteen feet. We weren't surprised because if Billy, being the oldest, had said he had found a home to put Pa in and Pa wasn't going to put up a fuss, we were gullible enough to believe him.

Sitting on the old sofa twelve feet from the hang-up hooks, he boasted, "Watch this," aiming for the hook. Eight inches off centre of the hook, he rung the clock. The clock got its wish anyway. It dropped six feet to the floor, engulfed in Billy's heavy woollen cap. We ran breathless to the crippled clock and inspected it. It wouldn't have surprised us if we had found blood.

All engines were stopped and the face was broken. What a lovely evening we had planned! And now we were running around with a dead clock, looking for a new face before Pa saw to it that we had new faces. A next-door neighbour cut glass for window panes and we soon smuggled the clock to him. He did a great job putting the glass in, but he said he wouldn't dare mess with the interior.

The first place Pa looked when he came into the house at any time of day was at the clock, no matter what was going on, even if the walls were being shaken by an earthquake. Time study would have been a good field for Pa to go into, because it seemed as if he was always checking the time it took his body to go from one place to another.

Murray phoned the operator before Pa arrived to start calling us at four a.m. again, to be informed that it was against the rules for her to phone us any more. We wondered if we should have her arrested, or hold off on the $2.40 a month, but Pa paid this by cash. It was a cool spring evening, five o'clock. We huddled together in search of a plan that would work. Pa would be home in minutes and he was going to look at the clock that wasn't working.

I could have practised juggling three oranges in front of it. But the only time we had three oranges in the house at one time was at Christmas; and we ate them before we got them.

We could have pretended we were practising for church and sing with great fervour "Onward Christian Soldiers," with wild swinging of arms to hide the tickless clock. The closer he got to the clock shelf, the louder we would get. But Pa had never heard us sing, never dreamt we could carry a tune.

Had he been close to the race track, Billy could have gotten us a set of blinders. But we'd look sort of suspicious trying to hold Pa's head erect to place the blinders on him. He wasn't used to us fooling around with his head and probably would have bucked us off and kicked us.

We wished we could have found a fast carpenter who could have built Teedy's body into the wall behind the clock with just his right arm sticking out, so he could regulate the small stems on the back of the stopped clock. But Teedy would have had to possess a very good feel for the exact length of a minute and he hardly knew minutes from days. (The only day Teedy really knew how to say proper was Tuesday, and if a caller was to ask him what time Pa would be home, Teedy would say Tuesday, even if it was Friday. He really messed up a lot of appointments.)

In our next idea, even though Teedy was all pepped up with enough deviltry left in him for three hours, we confiscated all this energy and put him to bed. He agreed with us as we rushed him up to the bedroom, still in daylight. It was his turn to bundle Pa off to the mine in the morning, so we made sure he took the useless clock with him.

Pa arrived and, through habit of checking the time, his first words were, "Where's the clock?" I said, "Well, Teedy was kind of sleepy, so he thought he'd go to bed, and he took the clock so he wouldn't have to get up and get it." We knew by the look on Pa's face that he was satisfied. We felt so happy, we nearly believed ourselves.

Luckily, a friend of Ma's was a jack-of-all-trades. His main work was to fix gramophones and old clocks. We were trying to figure out what to do to repay him when we remembered he had a small garden. We would pay him in manure. But for now, we had to get Pa to bed fast. He had his smoke, read his paper and then every time he looked at one of us three, we gave him a big, make-believe yawn like a hippopotamus. That would make Pa yawn. We eventually tired him out, since there were three big mouths against one. Pa went down to defeat, saying, "Take the kindlings out of the oven," as he padded along to bed. Giving him time to make an imprint on the old mattress, Billy sneaked upstairs to Teedy, who was dead awake and becoming more active to the point of whistling. Billy told him to cut out the whistling, at least until Pa fell asleep.

Teedy was glad to see Billy with the latest events, since along with his whistling he had just finished counting every nail that came through from the outside roof. A whispered "ninety-three" came from Teedy's lips. Once a slight snore was heard from Pa's room, Teedy wasn't long slipping his pants and gum rubbers on and lightly following Billy down the stairs. Billy, with a death grip on the crippled clock, was to go over to the clock-fixer's, even though it was eighy-thirty p.m., to tell him our troubles. The man stuttered a lot when he talked and sprayed spit all over the place. He used to come drunk to our house sometimes and many a time I heard Pa say to Ma, "It's bad enough trying to understand what it's saying when it's sober, but talking when it's drunk with all the new expressions on its face, I don't want to see it here. It makes me nervous."

Billy landed at his house and the man stammered a minute hello before he found out the trouble and that the job had to be done tonight. He had been busy working on a Victrola, so leaving that, he went to work on the Big Ben. A half-hour later, the clock was breathing again, some colour had come back to its face and the alarm had a healthier ring. It seemed ready to wake Pa right now and it was only nine o'clock.

Billy told him we'd give him two wheelbarrow loads of horse manure next day for his mother's flowerbed. He looked at Billy as if he'd overpaid him.

Billy, the clock-bearer, raced home. Three different-sized smiles met him at the door as he stepped in with a broader grin, saying, "It's fixed." The three of us escorted Teedy upstairs with the clock, so he wouldn't drop it. But we didn't have to worry. Teedy was carrying the Big Ben flat on his open palm and covering it with his other hand, as though it was a day-old chicken that he didn't want to fly.

At five a.m., having gotten Pa off to the mine, Teedy gave us a shove, saying, "Get up and get the horse manure," a sentence that's hard to decipher when one is awakened suddenly. For a few minutes, Murray thought that's what Pa was having for breakfast.

All of us got up before it was too bright and had our porridge and bread and molasses. Then Murray slipped over to Lyle's, our good neighbour next door, to borrow his wheelbarrow, to find he wasn't up. But that didn't disrupt our plans. Murray came back with Lyle's property and we headed for the fields. Horses were scarce around home, but in two hours we had a fine mixture of cow and horse manure. The man was so happy to see us emptying our second wheelbarrowful on the garden that he got out a big, "Thank you, boys," without a stutter, though we were sprayed a little.

Lyle's wheelbarrow was washed out and put back in his shed without him ever knowing we had borrowed it. We each had another small plate of porridge and thought what a nice feeling it was to hear Big Ben ticking off its seconds, safely sitting on its shelf, with a look on its new round face as if to say, "Pa will never find out how you broke my heart. My lips are sealed." And whenever Billy got the urge to ring anything, we urged him to do the wash that day. He could get lots of practice wringing out Pa's underwear, so his neck wouldn't be wrung by Pa.

5

Watergate Break-In...Grade One

In grade one, our reader got us into trouble time after time. When I wasn't reading it upside down, we were dropping it in mud puddles by mistake and getting ourselves into more hot water with Pa.

During our first taste of school, Murray and I were the sole owners of nothing but a small primer, purchased by Pa, which had a maple leaf on the cover. Pa would sooner have seen us come home with an ear missing than to hear that we had forgotten to take home our reader. To Pa it was like leaving your baby in the grocery store.

In school we usually had our reading lesson about an hour before going home for lunch. One morning just before dinner, Murray and I, the ones closest to the teacher, saw she was getting prepared to mark the lesson for the next day. She was standing beside us and, having left her reader on her desk, she reached down and picked up our book, while we stared daggers at her. She told the class how far down their lesson would be for the morrow. But how dare she touch the book Pa had paid for?

Our shoulders tensed, we gritted our teeth and our bodies stiffened as we kept a steady, worried eye on every bit of pressure she applied to our book. While I was thinking, "I hope she doesn't have any butter on her fingertips," (Pa hated fingerprints on his books) I almost snatched the book from her hands after she took her pen and marked the paragraph in our book.

This meant war. Why did she have to take our book? We only had one between us and there were two on every other desk. She then had the audacity to walk toward her desk, reading the short paragraph from our reader. At that point the buzzer for noon hour rang. We didn't care if it came and buzzed in our ears, we were watching every move she made with our book. She even plopped it down on her desk from a height of about a foot. She was really asking for it. Pa's warning thundered in our brains, "Take care of your book," as the kids lined up to go home to lunch. What he didn't tell us was that we'd have to wrestle with the teacher to get it back. And who could eat lunch at a time like this? It was the end of the world. We would have to stage a stunning robbery, a baby Watergate, in broad daylight.

The teacher didn't notice that Murray and I were now in shock. I was white and Murray was green, and we were both experiencing cold chills. I was having mini-blackouts and my focusing was off key. Normally we were the first in line, being the hungriest, but while the rest rushed to line up, we were the only two still sitting, dazed. We didn't have to voice our concerns to each other. Each of us was determined to get our book back if it meant a full scale investigation by the F.B.I., hopefully with the teacher going to prison for a few years.

Sluggishly, like we'd both just come down with a bad case of the flu, we tagged along at the end of the line, filled with resentment for the teacher we used to like before she stole Pa's reader. We desperately but quietly discussed our predicament as we marched from the room. Once out in the hall, we strode directly to the basement where the toilets were. We accomplished one act, but the second and most urgent was still ahead of us.

The janitor locked the school from noon to one o'clock, so we would have the whole school to ourselves. There would be no dinner for us today, but if we didn't retrieve our book there would be no more dinners for us any day until we could pay Pa back for the book. And what could five-year-olds do to make money? Maybe shine shoes. But most folks around home wore gum rubbers and they were shiny enough without us spitting on them.

After fifteen quiet minutes had elapsed, we scooted upstairs to our classroom and our stolen reader. We came to the main door to our classroom and ran into our first break-in problem. Murray and I were not much more than four feet tall, and a six-foot door with a small hook about six inches from the top separated us from our book. We thought about standing there until we grew to be six feet tall, but we'd have been there yet, because we're only 5' 9" today. I tried lifting Murray, but he was too fidgety and couldn't keep still. He said I was tickling him. It was probably lucky in one way that he couldn't reach the hook, because if he had unhooked it, the door would have flown open and Murray would have gone smack on his face with me landing on top of him. Then I would have had to tell the teacher that I killed Murray while playing Leap Frog.

With empty stomachs and time flying by, we were seriously considering flying when we came up with the solution. I would get down on all fours like a jackass, and Murray would stand on my back and reach the hook with no trouble at all, not even one flap of his wings.

Finally the deed was done and we were in the room. The book that Pa had bought for us was swiftly transferred from the teacher's desk to the inside crevice of our desk. We gave twin sighs of relief as we let ourselves out through the door and locked it again. Downstairs, we rushed to the toilets to await the arrival of the janitor and the rest of the kids.

At one o'clock, Murray and I merged with the other school kids, not telling a soul how we'd spent our noon hour. We were so relieved that we'd gotten our reader back that we weren't even hungry. The main bell rang and we lined up with the others and marched proudly into our room as if we'd just returned from a war we had won.

Every desk in the classroom had two books on top. Murray's and mine had nothing. "Class, be seated," came from the teacher who, we knew, had just had a lovely dinner. Planning to continue the lesson she had started before lunch, she asked, "Who took the book from my desk?" Our faces held looks of shocked disbelief and innocence which said, "Who would dare take a book off the teacher's desk?" With accusing eyes, we looked slowly around at the others in the class with expressions that said, "If we find the guy who took your book, we'll whomp the living daylights out of him." Murray even gave a suspicious glance to the back of the room where the janitor was sweeping the floor, while I threw a dirty look across the hall to the principal's office. Imagine the gall of some people!

Quietness reigned. Murray and I wished we were seated at the back of the class instead of right under the teacher's nose. "Now someone has taken the book," she continued. Not a purr from either of us. "Everyone look in your desks," she ordered. We wished we could have crawled into ours like moles and stayed there until school was over. Instead, our two heads bent simultaneously to look in the same desk, and we received mild concussions. Murray grabbed the book as if an escaped convict had just come in and planted it there to frame us. With incredulous eyes, he showed it to the teacher.

"How did it get there? It was on my desk when we left for lunch. Do you know, Andy?"

"No, miss," I answered very politely, since I was caught in a trap. I felt like saying, "Pa put it there." After all, it was Pa's fault.

"I want you and Murray to stay after school," the teacher said. Quite hungry by now on top of being scared, the thought of staying in after school gave us the same feeling as when Pa postponed our sentencing for some reason.

After school, in our explanation to the teacher, we poured out our tale of woe, punctuated with bursts of real tears. In high-pitched voices, blubbering uncontrollably, we stammered that Pa told us never to give the book to anyone, or lend it, or lose it, or leave it in school.

We could tell she sympathized with us. But we also knew that if she ever tried to get hold of our book again, she would have quite a tug-of-war on her hands, in which she'd be outnumbered three to one— her against Murray, me and Pa.

6

The Day I Turned Into A Russian

In grade one, the teacher used to give us a paragraph to read each night for homework. We would mark it with a faint x, and we were told not to read a bit further. So nothing and no one could get us to study what came next. After all, the teacher had told us how far down to read, and we were going to do just what she said. We were starting our school days with complete obedience— at least, the first part of grade one.

One Friday afternoon, the teacher told us to mark our lessons for Monday. The paragraph we were to learn ended in a question, which left Murray and me in a quandary for the whole weekend. The last line read, "I saw something on my way to school. Do you know what it was?" If there was ever a time our brains worked overtime, it was with this last line, and we talked of it for two whole days. My, my, what was it she saw? How could we wait until Monday morning? We should have gone to a fortune teller, or phoned the author of the book. We thought of everything imaginable trying to figure out what it was. It could have been a dead body, a spaceman, a vampire, or Pa, who was about the same as a vampire. We could have just asked an older brother or sister, but we didn't want to be disobedient to the teacher. But what could it have been?

About an hour before leaving for school on Monday, Murray called me aside to tell me he hadn't been able to stand it any longer, and that he had peeked at the line. He said, "I think I know what it was." I was mortified with the little cheat, but naturally wanted to hear what the object was that had ruined our weekend. Murray said, "It's a book." Yuck, so that's what the secret was. What a letdown. I felt like calling the teacher and telling her that the reader should be taken off the curriculum.

Feeling disenchanted and a wee bit guilty, we toddled off to school, where another surprise awaited us as we began the next lesson. It was not a book at all that the person had seen on her way to school, it was a brook, a word too big for Murray's vocabulary at that time, but certainly a lot more interesting to see than a book. Nevertheless, if things didn't take a dramatic upsweep in our reader stories, I knew one brook that was going to have one book thrown into it.

Now if you were able to read through your paragraph in class without stumbling too much, you received a gold or silver star. The teacher would paste the small paper star next to your paragraph, and how proud we were walking home from school, watching it glittering next to our lesson. The advantage Murray and I as twins had was that if only one of us got a star, the two of us could get credit for it from Pa. We often told him she gave us one for the both of us, because she was short on stars, and he usually fell for it. When neither of us got a star, we would draw on one and colour it as best we could. We counted on flashing it before Pa's eyes before he had a chance to put his reading glasses on, since Pa was never short on stars.

It was my turn to read this day; and once I had gotten under way, both the class and the teacher must have thought I was turning into a Russian. Murray also thought I was a bit loony, because he kept looking at me in astonishment. Even I had never experienced sentences like the ones I was spouting. I kept struggling through it, though, trying to do my best for that precious star, and thinking, "It's rough going, but I'm getting there." On I went, reading in pig latin, while the rest of the class tried to follow along with me.

I was wondering why there was such a commotion of pages turning. I thought that they must have been reading the wrong pages when I heard "Hold on, Andy" from the teacher. Hastily she left the room, telling me to remain standing. Soon she reappeared with three other teachers. At that moment I was thinking, "I'll merit two stars today, plus a medal for being bilingual."

"Continue reading, Andy," she said. All geared up from the small rest I had had while she was gone, I proudly continued my story which, if right side up, would have read, "Dear little red rose, may I pick you?" Without even suspecting it, I had been reading the story upside down, which meant I was reading from right to left instead of the normal way; and it might have worked had I been reading in Hebrew.

I still hadn't caught on to the fact that I was reading the book upside down, so it wasn't too hard for me to display my fine reading ability to those extra teachers and I sputtered on, "You pick I may, rose red little." By this time, I was beginning to suspect that the book had a trick story in it which was written in a foreign language and the teacher had chosen me to read it, and that I was doing so well in the strange tongue that she wanted others to appreciate my talent. At last, the teacher stopped me and told me the awful truth. I was flabbergasted. Why hadn't I looked on the cover before I started to read? Surely I would have noticed the maple leaf was upside down. But at the beginning of this chapter, there was a big, red rose with buds and stem, and it was hard to tell the bottom from the top.

Besides, I was so eager for that blessed star that I paid no attention to the position of the book and was quite disappointed when I didn't get one. But I guess you can't give someone a star for their ability to read upside down. When I told Pa I didn't get a star because I was reading the story upside down, he gave me a clout for standing on my head in school; I finally saw the stars I wanted to see so badly.

7

My Mumps Just Exploded

Short of nuclear disaster or the Second Coming, there were very few legitimate ways of getting out of school. But one of these ways was sickness. Any disease that was rampant, we were on guard, waiting for it to strike. We just knew we had to be next. There were too many of us for any disease to slip by. We were very schooled in identifying germs, too. Murray, my twin, could point across the street and tell you what kind it was, flu or diarrhoea.

One year every third family in town was down with the mumps, but no one at our house got it, not even Teedy, who had everything from hangnails to fits. We had all the symptoms memorized; the swelling glands, the sore throat. Why in heaven's name couldn't we catch it?

Walking home from school one afternoon, I began fingering a very sore spot on the side of my throat. The more I rubbed it, the larger and more tender it got. Finally my gland really began to swell, and I looked like a bullfrog full of song, or like someone had blown a bubble out of my neck.

My three brothers were at their happiest and thought I should have been presented to the King and knighted. But then His Majesty might have caught the mumps while he was dubbing me. They diagnosed my case. "Same way John Capp started with the mumps." They also knew some girl who had also started this way. With all my symptoms, Ma started worrying about the next step to take. Murray talked her into keeping the four of us home from school, telling her that if anyone in the family had mumps, the teacher would send you all home anyway and maybe have your parents imprisoned and injected with the bubonic plague.

It would be about ten days before the mumps left you, so Murray and the rest were expecting a glorious holiday all expenses paid, at my expense. I didn't put up much of a fuss either. Why, if it meant missing some school, I would have been willing to have a baby. I was so deliriously happy, I almost slipped and told Pa he wouldn't have to go to work in the mine for ten days. But I held my tongue. If Pa was at home for ten days with us, we would rather have gone to school covered from head to toe in mumps. I decided I didn't care if every miner in the pit got the mumps, even if they spread to the diamond mines in South Africa.

The lump was getting much larger, as if I had swallowed a baseball, and sorer. Finally, after two day's absence from school, I did have a baby of sorts. An explosion took place which sent the four of us right back to school. What had begun as a mump on my throat had turned into a large, blind boil, which came to a head on the second day, erupted like a volcano and disqualified all rights to the mumps.

It was quite hard for Ma to write the excuses for our absences. It wouldn't look right to say I had the mumps and was over them in only two days. The teacher would think I was superhuman, or that an alien craft had landed in our front yard and healed me instantly, or that I had ties with a witch doctor, or that Ma was a cruel person who sent me back to school still mumped up.

On the other hand, it would have been embarrassing to have to tell the teacher, "Please excuse Billy, Murray, Teedy and Andy for being absent Tuesday and Wednesday— Andy had a blind boil." The teacher might think that Ma thought my blind boil would cause a contagion of blind boils to run rampant throughout the school, like those boils in the Bible, and next would come the plague of locusts. Or she might think that my family had a thing for blind boils, loved them, worshipped them even, and that any time one of us had one, everyone stayed home to look at it, even Pa and the dog.

So after a meeting behind closed doors, unseen by Pa, Ma decided to say she'd kept us home to do some work; and off I strolled to school with a very noticeable blob of iodine over my mumpy boil, and my three locust brothers swarming along beside me, like baby bees.

8

Wet Kisses

When I was a teenager, there was nothing more romantic than a full moon shining on Sydney Harbour and the temperatures reaching into the seventies.

On this particular night, I had a blind date. The girl I was supposed to date chummed around with a very beautiful girl; a buddy of mine tried many times to have a date with this beauty, only to have her girlfriend (my blind date) tag along the full night.

Earlier in the day my friend told me he had dated the lovely Cora and she always had a girl called Myrtle with her. He asked me pleadingly, "Do you think you can tear them apart, so I can see Cora alone?"

"What does Myrtle look like?" I asked.

"She's average, a little on the hefty side. She's not bad. But you don't have to marry her, Andy, just take her out this once and get her off my hands."

In the event she was the least bit sexy, I said, "Okay, just this once." Jim said, "Good," and told me to meet him at seven o'clock.

Dressed to the high heavens, by suppertime I had so much love in my heart for this person I had never before laid eyes on that I could hardly eat. What a vision of loveliness I had conjured up. I mean, just how ugly could the friend of a beautiful girl be? At least half of Cora's beauty would have to rub off on Myrtle, wouldn't it? I could see her in my mind's eye; long blond hair, blue eyes, figure like Venus, graceful, intelligent, kind and loving. I just hoped she didn't want to marry me tonight. I might have said 'yes' and then I'd have to divorce Pa and leave a panful of dirty dishes, as it was my turn to do the housework.

Off I trotted to meet Jim for my big date, which would probably change my life. "They'll be along pretty soon," said Jim. "The light just went out in Cora's room."

Combing my hair and straightening my tie, my heart was beating faster and I was starting to get nervous. Besides this, I could see Jim had a guilty look and wanted to tell me something I wasn't going to like, something like, "I know you'll despise her like I do."

The two girls came out the front door of the house and met us on the street. It was hard to get a good look at Myrtle because the street lights were ten hydro poles apart and we were walking four abreast like in the army. I should have hollered 'two steps back' like a sergeant major, so she'd take the hint. But as it was, I almost had to force her back with me, she was so closely connected to Cora.

I still didn't have much of a peek at her face. I could see Jim's girlfriend's beautiful face because she turned to me when they came out of the house and said, "Andy, this is Myrtle." I almost gagged on her name. We had a hen named Myrtle. I'll bet she would have liked to know I was comparing her to our hen.

The first streetlight was what I was waiting for. It shone on her like a spotlight. It was then I found I had no prize, except the booby prize. She wore a heavy red jacket and a butterfly skirt, very sexy from the rear. But from the front there was something missing. She was much stouter than me, with that motherly look and spread. Her hair, a golden colour, built up her looks some, but was wasted on her. There was one tooth missing for every two that were standing and I could see she didn't brush three times a day. She seemed to slobber each time she laughed, which wasn't often, thank heavens. And me so pretty. Soon, Cora and Jim went on their own way, leaving Myrtle and me alone.

She had the knack of making me feel like her son even though, according to her, she was younger than me. Every time I'd do something like kick a stone (and to break the monotony, I kicked many), she said, "That will bring on varicose veins." Then one time I sneezed and she said, "Try not to sneeze more than five times, because ten to one your heart will stop." She went on to tell me how her Aunt Flora had died sneezing. I began thinking what a lovely way to enjoy the moonlight, with her telling me what I should and shouldn't do to keep on living. Every so often she would gaze longingly up at the moon like she was getting ready to howl at it like a banshee.

While we were walking through the park, she surprised me for a minute when she reached in her pocket and struggled to get something out. At first I thought she might have been pulling a gun to shoot us both. Instead, she came up with a package of cigarettes. If you took a survey at the time, there were only about a handful of women in our town who smoked, and my date was one of them. So for the next half an hour I watched her through a haze of blue smoke as she puffed her way through half the pack. And she was telling me how to keep living.

Heading for another light, she made a complete turn, saying, "I live over there," pointing to a dimly lit house which should have been haunted, and probably was. There were parts of cars and trucks strewn around the yard like a car repair shop. In the seats of the old cars were many pairs of florescent eyes, watching eagerly to see if we were going their way. Myrtle said, "Those are a few of my cats. I have twelve." I put my hand in to pet one of them and it hissed and clawed at my hand. Myrtle told me it was my fault the cat had scratched me, because I pulled my hand back so fast. It was turning into quite a date. Then she said, "I have to go in the house for a minute. You stay here until I come out." I thought, "Oh good, maybe she's going in to take her mask off."

Instead, in a few minutes she was pulled out through the door and almost rushed off her feet by a Saint Bernard as big as a small dinosaur. I wished she had put him in the car with the cats to see how they got along with each other. Breathlessly, she said she was going to walk him. Run him would have been more like it. I told her it was a shame she didn't bring her cats along, too, then people would think we were the Pied Pipers of Cape Breton.

She had a thirty-foot rope tied to the beast's collar, as if she was going to lower him down a well. If she had that dog along for protection from me, he was going to have an easy night of it, because I was at least five feet from her and Fido, stepping smartly along at all times, and planning to keep it that way. Even without the dog, she'd have been safe.

The three of us strolled along under the moon, Myrtle and I at times looking as if we were trotting our cow out to pasture. Jim had been gone for an hour, off somewhere embracing his darling. And here I was with a woman made for dogs. I knew my night was going to be a dud as she and I and the dog and rope sauntered along. Why, I could have had more fun at home watching Pa and Blanche put a new set of grates in the coal stove.

The moon must have been getting to Myrtle because she reached over and took my hand. Well, I didn't worry too much about that because I had another one, but the dog kept staring me in the face. At this moment, she stooped over and kissed the dog on its big, drooling mouth. Of course, the dog didn't mind because Myrtle had a few frothy slobbers on her mouth from supper. They made an ideal couple.

Then Myrtle said, "You know, if I pretended you were grabbing me (this had to be wishful thinking on her part), Buster would jump you and tear you to shreds."

Neither she nor Buster would have to worry about that. I would rather have grabbed Pa and had him tear me to shreds. It was then I took my hand back and made sure I kept it from ever straying within her grasp again.

Next we sat on a brick fence for a bit with the dog between us and yards of rope curled up like a lasso at Myrtle's feet, while she told me all the dog's habits; what it was fed, how she fed it, what she fed it in, what hours of the day it picked for its toilet habits, where she took it for a walk and for how long, how deep its bark was, and where its father lived. She told me everything about the dog except why she looked like one.

I said to her, "You know, some night you'll be walking that thing and it will see a cat and take off after it right up a hydro pole. You'll still be holding the rope and you'll be slung over the tension wires and burnt to a crisp." She let out a big guffaw, like Mortimer Snurd, sprayed me with spit, then bent down, saying, "Not my baby," as both slobbered a kiss again. Little did she know, I almost wished it would happen at that minute.

54

Tired of Myrtle and the dog talking everything over between themselves, I suggested we walk down to the shore and watch the tide, which was ready to turn. Now I don't know why I bothered trying to take care of her, but I told her again it wasn't too smart to wrap the dog's rope around her wrist, in case he took off on her. And again she said, "My dog doesn't do things like that."

No sooner did the words burst from her lips when a shore rat, as large as a well-fed tomcat, peeked up from behind a huge stone in front of us. The dog, without pardons, took off at a terrific speed, dragging Myrtle along the stony shore like a sled over bare ground. I ran to her assistance amidst Myrtle's groans and Fido's loud barking. I pulled back on the rope to get some slack so she could get her bruised wrist clear. Her skirt and blouse were torn, her knees were cut and bruised, and her golden hair, the only good part of her, was a mass of tangles from her slide over the sandstone.

She blamed me for taking her and Fido down to the shores because Fido was not used to the shores at night. Meanwhile, the dog, still in the distance, eventually spent his energy without getting the rat and came trotting back to his messed-up momma.

Back up the path near Myrtle's house, we were sitting on the fence counting stars when she spoke up and said, "Oh, I left my purse down on the shore." It was a quarter-mile back to the shore, so I jumped at the chance to get clear of her for half an hour or so.

Back on the shore I found her purse. Picking it up, it was extra heavy, so I thought I'd glance through it and see what she had in it. I found a plastic bag with a good-sized bone for Fido, a small bag of candy, probably Fido's too, a dog brush and a dog book. I wouldn't have been a bit surprised if I would have found a chapter turned down called "How to Marry a Dog."

Sauntering back along the shore, I could hear loud voices a little ways off coming from up where I'd left Myrtle. As I climbed the steep path up the cliff, I could see a male figure silhouetted in the moonlight coming toward me at a snappy pace. I started to run to meet whoever it was to see what the commotion was. Meeting the figure on top of the cliff in a neighbour's back yard, I could see it was Jim. He looked wild-eyed like a maniac. Hollering and screeching something about Myrtle, he grabbed me by the front of my shirt and threw me up against a tree. As I fought him off, I started thinking Jim's date with Cora couldn't have gone very well. In that two or three hours with her he'd gone completely berserk. He must have been trying to tell me he'd rather have Myrtle instead. He wouldn't get much of a fight over that.

I was at the point of screaming for a neighbour to come help, in case Jim tried to push me off the cliff or whip out a hidden knife. Then as he said, "What did you do to Myrtle?" I began to put things together.

I started to laugh then and Jim thought I'd gone crazy. I laughed out the words, "I didn't do anything. The dog did it." Then I explained to him about Myrtle's rocky slide by dog team. And Jim began to laugh. I told him he didn't have to worry about my romantic inclinations towards Myrtle, that I was more attracted to the dog than to her.

Then Jim began to tell me what had happened when he and Cora arrived back. Seeing Myrtle there full of scratches, torn clothes and with her hair all dishevelled, he jumped to conclusions before Myrtle could explain her appearance and the reason she was there alone. Jim thought I had taken off before the police arrived.

Jim knew that he could never ask me to double date with him again. I wouldn't have gone with him if he'd said my girl looked like Helen of Troy. Not only that, he could tell by the look on my face that I would never do him any favours whatsoever, in this life or the next; and he knew he was getting off easy.

He'd either have to marry Cora that night or put up with the trailing arbutus on his future dates. Myrtle walked home with Cora, the dog trailing behind them, looking back at me as if to say, "You're lucky. I may have to put up with another wet kiss before I go to bed for the night."

Jim and I walked home and I asked him who I had the date with anyway, Myrtle or the dog. He just laughed and said, "Thanks, Andy, you broke the spell. Tomorrow night Cora is going to sneak away from Myrtle (she'd have to chloroform her) and meet me in town."

This incident left a lasting impression on me and I'm very wary of Saint Bernards, especially those on long ropes. And

I'm quite nervous about looking up at the face of the owner. It might be Myrtle and who knows, she might forget about the dog, old droopy drools, and fall completely in love with me, and then we'd drool kiss forever.

9

No Chocolates for You

When we were young, just the word 'chocolate' meant heaven to us, as we knew we'd never own a box. So one Christmastime when I was trying to make a penny, I came across an ad that tempted me. It coaxed like this:

> Make money for Christmas in your spare time. (As if we ever had any.) Pick your lucky sweetheart's name. Pull out tab and you have a chance from one cent to fifty-nine cents to win a box of chocolates.

The seller (if you wish to call me that) would receive a pocket watch and chain for selling all the cards, plus a pen and pencil set for promptness. Did I fall for this enticement! The only time I ever ate anything even resembling chocolate was when a truck came by one day passing out free samples of Ex-Lax. I told the driver there were three families living in our house and then ate all three boxes. (Though many years ago, I still have belated symptoms, rather regularly.)

Anyway, the chocolate company began sending me punch cards. The punch cards were rectangular, about 4"x7" and had female names on small, round tabs. Under each flap, after the buyer had picked his favourite girl's name, there were prices ranging from one to fifty-nine cents, which the puncher was to pay me. (Little did I know that the punchers would soon become the punchers, literally, while I was to become the punchee.) After I sent the chocolate company all the money I took in from the punches along with each person's address, everyone who had bought a punch was to receive a two-pound box of chocolates from the company.

It was easy to sell the punches for half the card, where the smaller amounts of money existed under the little flaps, because after being scientifically analyzed under a 25 watt bulb, like those Lotto crooks in Quebec a few years ago, they were picked by everyone in our family. Even aunts we didn't know before joined the bonanza of the low flaps to get that coveted box of chocolates. If by accident one of our family pulled a high number, Billy and I, working like the mafia, would lather the little flap back down with just a pin point of molasses on each side (took a good day to dry). Then we'd turn to the relative and say, "That will be two cents instead of fifty-nine."

There was always a stalemate after selling the first half of the punch cards. People seemed to have a premonition that the high numbers were the only ones left and were leery to pick a punch.

And to make matters worse, something was telling me that I had better take stock of my small change can, which was in full view of my heathen brothers, whom I trusted. But every day the bottom of the can was coming more and more into view. One day I caught Billy barehanded reaching in, but he soon made me believe he was just counting it like the King in his counting house, as if he were my treasurer. Then from time to time Teedy or Murray made a slip and said they liked the Mickey Mouse cartoon. It was then I went and checked my can, knowing the only time they would get to see the show was when they passed by its doors. Also, I had been making a few trips to the show myself and they never let me in free.

As I said before, once a person had paid for a punch, it was my responsibility to see that they got their chocolates. Fat chance. At times I felt that I should give the money back to the ones who punched, but after looking over my names and who needed it the most, I came to the conclusion that nobody needed the money more than me.

My biggest mistake was selling one to a policeman and knowing as soon as he poised his fingers over the little flap he was a fifty-niner. I just had to return his money. But what a job I had trying to get that amount. I sold the only mirror in our house to a secondhand store for fifteen cents, and a poker and lifter for thirty-three cents, although Pa still had the bill for ninety-eight cents where he'd just bought them at the Co-op. Next, I took an all out chance and sold our only dustpan for eleven cents, paid off the mortgage, then lied gracefully to the police that the chocolates were limited and the supply had run out.

My cheap punch customers kept bugging me for their chocolates, and I was thinking seriously of hanging myself, but I had on Billy's new shirt, unbeknownst to him, and it would have been soiled. How could I give them chocolates with only a few dimes in the bottom of my cup and one which had to be used to see a Tarzan movie? I would gladly have lain down and given them two quarts of my blood instead. I even thought I might try a recipe for chocolates and give them that (if only I had saved the Ex-Lax), along with the phone number of our doctor. But I was only good at molasses candy, and even then I forgot to grease the plate.

Since I wasn't making any more fifty-nine cent sales, I could see my brothers weren't as friendly towards me. They kind of ignored me now with looks of disgust on their faces. Everything went against me along with the disappearing money. I couldn't even send the company back their card because my sister threw my pants in the old galvanized wash tub, punch card and all. If only I'd been in those heavy pants at the time of the washing, I could have saved those large number tabs, or I might have been lucky enough to have been drowned and done with it all.

When the pants dried out, I reached into the damp hind pocket and produced something resembling a piece of damp, speckled bark. This was what I was supposed to turn in with the right amount of money to receive my promptness gift. But what now? Should I send the company my chilled pants with the card in the pocket, so they could see "this has to be true," and possibly send me a pair of jeans with waterproof pockets and an indestructible card, plus a small pamphlet on "How to Get Through Life Though Jinxed."

What a time I had dodging the people who had pulled high punches and were still waiting for their chocolates. Every day I had to pass this guy's house I'd sold a fifty-nine cent punch to. If I was talking to a friend, my voice would change, I would begin to stutter, and I'd start walking sideways, just waiting for a voice to call out, "Hey there, where are my chocolates?" This went on for months. I should have left for South America, but with my luck, I would probably have come face to face with an Aztec I owed some chocolates to.

My customers began to look like my punch card, with small oval heads that contained the number 59. It seemed like the whole population of Cape Breton had bought punches from me. There was nothing to be done unless I spent the rest of my life in a gorilla suit.

Finally, I could take it no longer, so Billy and I staged an elaborate accident in the schoolyard where I fell off a swing and got amnesia. After this, everybody forgot about me and their chocolates. However, the chocolate company didn't forget about me. I should have sent Billy to their head office to knock them off their swings so they would get amnesia.

Letters began arriving from the company, secretly opened and hidden. One really had me worried. It said a representative would be sent to the school after me, though with my attendance record, ten to one I wouldn't be there. He probably would have found me at the shore, but I might have drowned him.

These letters went on for over two months. Each day I'd rush to the mail so I could destroy the evidence. One day in school, a loud rap came at the door. A man asked for Andy MacDonald. I slumped to the door, wishing I had attended school that day under an assumed name, wearing a false face. I was ready to accept the striped pyjamas and the ball and chain. Instead, the janitor handed me a small brown reader I'd been looking for for days, which he'd found down behind a toilet. Eventually the chocolate letters blew over. But today I feel guilty eating chocolates. I feel I should be sending them to my customers in Cape Breton.

10

My First Good Slug

Pa was a tee-totaller (and me too), so we never saw any beer or liquor around the house, except for the time when we made our own wine. Whenever I saw old-timers take a drink behind buildings or in cars, I had the impression that as soon as they glugged back that first swig they were instantly drunk, turning into Mr. Hyde and capable of murder. So before they tipped the bottle back, I made sure I was well out of the way.

One day when I was about eight, a buddy of mine asked me if I would go to town with him on an errand for his mother, a thin-framed alcoholic. He coaxed me with some candy. I didn't need much coaxing anyway, and would probably have gone with him even if he'd offered me poison ivy, because it was always a treat, especially in wintertime, to get inside a strange house, maybe to get some cookies or bread and molasses and a chance of heat.

Skipping up the driveway toward the house, I could hardly wait for the crooked-framed door to open to see what kind of goodies awaited me inside.

We knocked lightly and a sloppy, heavy-set woman in her fifties, reeking of heaven-knows-what, and who might have been Frankenstein's mother, opened the squeaky door about three inches and glared into our faces. Convinced her callers in no way resembled the police (we instead looked like two of the Seven Dwarfs— Sleepy and Dopey) and picking her teeth with her fingers, she asked us who our fathers were. Right then I was ready to run for home. I didn't want to mention Pa's name in case he found out I was visiting a bootlegger. So I mumbled something tough about Pa being Attila the Hun, which wasn't that far from the truth. After she found out my friend's mother's name, a long, fat arm reached out and with a lion's grip yanked us both in together like stuffed toys.

Watching the chunky arms snap hooks and locks on the old door, I knew I wouldn't live to taste any goodies. She was the witch in "Hansel and Gretel." My pal wasn't afraid at all, and he didn't seem the least bit disturbed as he passed her a scrunched up dollar bill, while I was thinking she must have hypnotized him. Reaching under the uneven cupboard, probably to bring out a long, shiny knife with which to do us in, she asked him about my background. I wondered if I should tell her the tale of the King of England owing my twin and me five hundred dollars, but I decided against it because by the look of her she would have kidnapped me and written the King for ransom.

Each time she looked at me, I went into a fit of shivering like I was being electrocuted, but I remained in front of her with my head bowed like a humble servant waiting for my orders.

The old cook stove glowed a dull red, much the same as her face, and easily noticeable in the gloomy kitchen. Maybe she planned to kill us both that way, I thought, still noticing the similarity between her, her stove and the witch in "Hansel and Gretel." (And she hadn't even offered us any gingerbread.) I expected her at any moment to grab us and slam us into her roasting hot oven. I even tried to stand crooked so she couldn't get as good a grip on me as if I stood straight. Anyway, I figured she'd start on him first because he had more meat on him. All I'd amount to would be a couple of pretzels.

I'd already picked my line of escape and inched my way closer to the door. A large rat hole would have done. I know I could have slithered through it as long as I jumped out of my gum rubbers.

Pushing the faded curtain on the cupboard back into place, she now gripped a Coca-Cola bottle in her ham-like hand. Holding the neck with her thumb and digit finger, she walked toward me. Ah ha, a Molotov cocktail was how we were to go. I moved quickly behind my hypnotized friend before she threw it, waiting for the fatal 'kaboom' and knowing I would probably blow out through her roof and come to rest on the hydro wires like a lost kite.

"Why did we ever come here in the first place," I thought. I then came to the conclusion that my buddy must have wanted to die, maybe because he couldn't take the cold Cape Breton winters, and he was going to take me with him to the great Pa-less world in the sky. But what a way to go! Fried to a crisp. And here I'd been thinking I was going to get some cookies.

She peeked out under the bottom of the drawn blind, on the lookout no doubt for any witnesses to our murders. Like a sheep being led to the slaughter, I whispered to my pal, "Is there another door?" He looked at me like he didn't know who I was and as if I was speaking to him in a new language. It had to be the hypnosis or else he was in shock, like me. But I wasn't shocked enough not to plan an alternate exit. I was now sizing up the attic above my head, in case I took an instant fly. I'm sure that while I had been imprisoned in her house, I had developed springs on the soles of my feet; if worse came to worse, I could bounce right out through her roof like a kangaroo.

The evil fat one left the window and strode directly to the cook stove. Still gripping the bottle, she opened the warming closet, moved a few dish towels, reached in and brought out an aluminum teapot with steam pouring from its spout like a vapour trail. This is it! She's going to poison us. I wished she'd make up her mind. It was hard on an eight-year-old's heart not knowing which way he was to go.

Pouring the cola-coloured liquid into the bottle, the steam prevented it from filling to the brim. Next I began to wonder why my buddy had taken me way up to this monster's house just to get tea, when our teapot at home always had some old tea in it which we usually threw out. The witch then reached into a dirt-stained cup, came up with a cork, stuck it in the bottle, then took another suspicious look out the window, like she was Ma Barker watching for the Feds, and at me at the same time with the same eye. Just as I was getting ready to make a mad dash for the exit, a strong, steady knock came on the door.

The wild-faced woman snatched the bottle from my pal's hand and shoved it under the sink, then grabbed a few dish towels and covered up the teapot in the warming closet. The knocks grew louder and more insistent. "Just a minute," she hollered, as she whispered orders in a raspy voice for me to crawl under her bed. She shoved my buddy into an old closet, saying, "When I open that door, I don't want either of you to even breathe."

Who was at the door? Pa? As soon as she left the bedroom, I whispered to my friend, "Get under here with me." In seconds he was next to me. "Who do you suppose it is?" I asked him. "It must be the police." When he said that, there was no need for anyone to worry about me making a noise. I froze solid, thinking of jail and hanging and Pa. "Just stay put," he whispered. "They'll just look around for a few minutes and leave."

Two chamber pots were situated under the bed with us. She had strategically placed them both in front of me so no one would suspect that behind them was a young kid who was almost dead of fright. When my buddy crawled under with me, he rearranged the pots as though he was a professional juggler, saying, "I was under here one other time." And it was then that he told me in a soft whisper that he had visited this awful woman twice a week for the past year.

Harsh voices came from the kitchen. We heard doors slam and drawers being opened and closed. After what seemed like hours, the door to her bedroom opened. We stopped breathing and blinking as one of the three policemen looked in the closet my friend had just transferred from. Then he looked quickly under the bed just as another policeman entered. When he noticed the large pots filled with a yellow liquid, he said, "Someone's bladder must be shot. She's got two pots."

Both of us were flat out way under the back of the bed and perfectly still. The policemen searched the entire house and we could hear them leaving. I was ready to get out from my cramped position under the bed, but my buddy said, "Stay there. She'll come in and tell us when the coast is clear." Soon we could hear her clamping down on the locks again, and then she entered the doorway of the bedroom and said, "Get out from under there." I didn't have to be told twice as I rolled out swiftly, sloshing half the contents of both pots over my buddy. Served him right anyway for getting me into this predicament. I was still deathly scared as she escorted us to the kitchen and handed my buddy his bottle.

I didn't allow her within arm's length of me as she waddled us to the door; I stayed glued behind my friend. I thought, "She'll have to get through him first if she tries to bash me with something, and at the same time I can kick her in the shins."

The only time I got ahead of them both was when she unshackled the bolts and locks. Then, like a thoroughbred sprinting from its gate, I was the first through the door. Speeding from the witch's abode and entering the atmosphere, I took giant steps on my springs, as if I were measuring off her property in acres.

I couldn't wait to ask my pal why he had paid her a dollar for a bottle of tea. Laughing, he said, "That's not tea. That's rum."

"Rum," I hooted. "You're crazy! She poured it right from the teapot." He insisted it was rum, but still not believing him, I grabbed the bottle, uncorked it and took a flowing mouthful, 'glug, glug, glug'. I flew backward as if shot, while he raced toward the uncorked bottle trickling the fiery fluid to the ground beside me. Strongest tea I'd ever tasted! I'd been weaned on tea and it had never affected me like that.

For several minutes I had no breath, no hearing, no sight and, I believe, no hair. I began gurgling and then vomiting and I couldn't stop. My pal felt like laughing, but he was too scared, not because of my health, but because of the half-full bottle of rum he'd have to give to his mother. After I was as dry as a dandelion gone to seed, he helped me up and we easily remedied the spilled rum. Passing the town's horse trough that was bubbling water like the Fountain of Youth, he held the uncorked bottle while I cupped the water into the neck, and in no time the dark liquid took on a weak tea look, which was what I thought it was in the first place.

His mother was loaded when we arrived at his house. She hugged the bottle closer to her, reached for a rum-stained cup and poured herself a drink without ever knowing the difference.

I told Pa about my adventure and was forbidden to go to this guy's house again, or even chum around with him. But Pa didn't have to worry about that, because I told my friend that if he ever asked me to go there with him again, even if he tried to bribe me with an entire candy store and ice cream parlour to boot, I'd have him arrested— by Pa.

But Pa was lucky I had made it home at all. He could have received word from a stranger, saying, "I'm sorry to have to tell you this, Mr. Pa, but Andy was found roasted, poisoned and blown to smithereens in the home of a bootlegger." Then not only would Pa mourn my loss, but it would leave him with the impression that I had died an alcoholic at the tender age of eight. Then he would come to find me wherever my smithereens had ended up, so he could trounce me again.

11

Duck Muck

Sanitation laws in our day were lenient. A person could have sewage running from their upstairs window into the neighbour's yard, out onto the highway and right into a grocery store without anyone raising a stink. This was the case in our town. Just a few hundred feet from our house a neighbour's sewage drain followed a path out to a roadside ditch. And did it ever stink, especially with six happy ducks wallowing around in it all day, bubbling up the scent. Many years of this steady flow of muck made the ditch wide and deep. This ditch was a shortcut for many families; however, jumping its four-foot width in the dark without hitting the mess was quite a feat.

One day in April, my twin, Murray, and I were invited to a girl's birthday party, which was to be held in about four days. The party was to start at seven o'clock. With this late night party we had the feeling of adulthood, and for days in advance we preened ourselves like hens for the auspicious occasion. We could feel ourselves becoming more handsome as each meal was digested.

By the way, we thought the girl whose birthday party it was was an angel. One of our favourite outfits she used to wear to school was a small blue skirt with two loops over the shoulders like braces, only much sexier than the braces we used to hold up our trousers. (Most of the time we had a torn brace dangling down around one hip like a runaway horse.)

At school we tried every pose, smile, walk and mannerism to have her fall for us so we could hold one of her wings. What a beauty! And here she was inviting us to her fifteenth birthday. Would we live? And more important, were twins allowed to marry the same angel? If I could have gotten a job,

I think I could have paid Murray off, as he was a lover of money. But there wasn't much of a chance of me making any money unless I started counterfeiting; that wasn't too likely since the only extra paper we had lying around was used in the outhouse.

Our oldest sister in Boston had sent Murray and me each a pair of white cotton pants and a pair of low sneakers, which were the first we had ever seen in our lives and, I believe, the first to be made since the creation of the world. Pa, of course, took possession of our gifts, saying, "Now you fellows wear those only on special occasions." Naturally, 'special occasions' for Pa meant our funeral, or possibly if we became world golfers, or diplomats sent by the Prime Minister to London to speak to King George about his bad habits, or Good Humour men, or ambulance drivers, or stand-ins for Ben Casey, or even if we were to become dental assistants, mixing up concoctions for fillings so as to speed up the patients' cavities.

Now the angel's birthday party didn't fall under any of those categories. But Pa must have suffered a wave of amnesia and forgot who we were, because he gave us the go ahead signal to wear our new togs to the party two days before it came to pass. This two-day advance notice was a godsend to get us in the mood. You couldn't count the number of times we scrubbed our bones and brushed our teeth.

Murray's toothbrush had coal black bristles and all because some Newfoundland woman had told him that coal soot would give lustre to the teeth. (I believe it was the same old woman who told us to splash our faces every morning with the dew that landed in the cowflaps overnight as a sure-fire remedy to get rid of our freckles.) Anyway, our old coal stove smoked more than Pa smoked his pipe, and small bubbles of soot had formed on the inside of the stove covers. This, she said, was supposed to be ideal to make the teeth sparkle. But all it did was make Murray look like Uncle Remus. Maybe that was the secret. You darkened your face up so badly trying to get soot on your teeth that in contrast to your black face, your teeth looked much brighter.

Once finished with cleansing our bodies and teeth inside and out, we practised walking without a sway. We didn't wear the pants around the house, but looked at them frequently, hanging leisurely over a steel hanger, waiting for the big night when the twin movie stars were to make their debut at the house of the angel.

Why, even our best friends wouldn't know who we were for a few minutes, especially if they looked at us from the sneakers up to our completely over-hauled heads, with our teeth twinkling like the Hope diamond.

Ma's gift to us for our first late night party was to make us each a homemade blouse with a string that you tied around the waist. And with our red bow ties we looked like waiters at a restaurant in Greece. We were most admirable to anyone of the opposite sex, even animals or people from other planets. We were gorgeous and we knew it. Sometimes I wondered how Murray could keep from saying, "Andy, I can't help it, but have you looked in the mirror lately? You're handsome."

I know we didn't sleep the night before the party. The next day after supper we had the pants and sneakers on, walking up and down the driveway in a semi-trance, especially with no sleep the night before. This was to be our wedding night, or at least the night we proposed to the angel. We were madly in love not only with her, but also with ourselves in our new garb. The moon came up early, but jealously went back under a cloud when it noticed how gorgeous we were.

It was a dark night and we were ready to float that joyous mile to Betty's. The ice and snow had thawed considerably the past few weeks and it felt almost muggy, a perfect night for love. Side by side, down the path we strode with devil-may-care swaggers, until we neared the sewage ditch. Murray stopped dead and halted me. Then, through the blackness of the night, Murray took his big jump. "Good," he says, "I'm over. Take a big leap, Andy." What Murray should have done was held me cradled in his arms like a baby and leaped over holding me. "Stand back out of the way," I answered. "Geronimo," I hollered. It seemed I broad-jumped thirty-two feet, only to land with a splash dead centre, knee-deep in duck muck.

Murray's pants got quite splattered when he helped me out, but I was a complete write-off. My biggest loss was my left sneaker, which hadn't ascended with my right one. If only I had landed on two ducks, I could have slid across to the other side on their backs as if I was on water skis. For half an hour we searched for my sneaker in the darkness, through the goo. Finally, what looked like a Brazilian toad came into sight, with molten lava flowing over its sides.

Fortunately, I was reluctant to wipe myself off with Betty's gift, which Murray carried, a fifteen cent box of handkerchiefs. About half a mile ahead, under a pale light, we checked our attire. I looked like I had on two pair of pants; a white pair fitting my waist, and a black pair covering my legs. I should have been playing hockey for the Blackhawks. I was a two-toned job, a stinking mess, and I cried inwardly. Murray, with his speckled pants, looked like a dalmatian puppy. We decided to continue on to the party because we'd heard Betty sneeze occasionally in school, so we knew she would like our handkerchiefs. In fact, we worshipped her so much we wouldn't have cared if she had sneezed in our mouths. But we were realistic enough to believe that the wedding would be off unless we told her we had just escaped from kidnappers who'd held us hostage in an outhouse.

Then we began to worry about what Pa would do to us when he got wind of our pants and the fact we had been attacked by a cesspool overseered by a duck. We would either have to live the rest of our lives at Betty's house, perhaps as her butlers, or leave on a safari for Africa.

Luckily for me but not for her, a distant aunt on Pa's side lived close to Betty's. Smelling as though I had just crawled out of a manure pile, I stunk to attention while Murray rapped. She opened the door, wishing she hadn't, as she said, "What in heaven's happened?" figuring we had just returned from the trenches in a war zone when Murray moved aside to give her the full throttling smell of my person in person.

"The damn duck ditch," was all I could murmur. She backed up, caught her breath and moved hastily away from me. "Take them off, child. Take them off," she kept repeating as she turned on all the faucets and opened all the windows. Then she handed me a sexy skirt of hers to put on while I was waiting for my vile smelling pants. Cool and airy, I waited while Murray looked on. He had a few irregular spots of goo on his pants, but far enough apart so as not to cause concern and leaving people to think he was wearing polka dot pants, quite uncommon in the white duck pants industry.

While I had on her skirt, waiting for the wash-up, a neighbour came in to fix her faucets. He had never seen us before. About twenty years older than us, he could hardly keep his eyes off me. I saw the love lights in his eyes as he looked at my slim waist and forgotten breasts. You could tell he thought Murray was my steady as Murray's big eyes made signs for me to lock my legs together while sitting so the plumber couldn't see my stale underwear.

We knew the party had started as Aunt Rosa hissed the hot iron up the left leg of my steaming pants. Murray was still waiting for me, not one bit enthraled by my aunt's checkered skirt like the plumber was. I hurriedly changed into my pants, and now with dampened pockets I gave off a different odour. My aunt had sprinkled me with dashes of creolin, as if she was throwing vinegar over a bed of lettuce. I guess she thought the disinfectant might prevent duck muck fever.

Murray and I arrived at the party about twelve minutes late, unfortunately for the party-goers who, once they'd got a whiff of us, wished we'd arrived twelve days late. Betty the angel's mother was the recipient of the shaky knock on the door as Murray and I stood erect and embarrassed. "The twins," she announced, and we noticed her nostrils bulge in and out like a horse getting ready to whinny. Wishing I was encased in a plastic bubble, I thought, "My heavens, she's smelled me already." Murray smelled a shade better than me, so I stayed behind him most of the night. Then I figured if I could sit on my legs, the smell wouldn't be so overwhelming, but there again, where were my manners in my future mother-in-law's house, with me sitting around all night in a lotus position like Swami Maharishi Yogi.

The odour I gave off was sort of a Lestoil smell. Very few girls sat near me and the ones who did moved the instant they sat down, as if they had squatted on a pin cushion. They kept muttering hushed sentences and shying away to other seats on the opposite side of the room, while I was wishing I could fly up on the chandelier, and that maybe the odour would rise to the ceiling like heat. But if that was the case, the odour that was in the room should have lifted everyone to the ceiling as if we were all on magic carpets. If only someone had come up with a game that would have taken over an hour to play, one where everyone put on blindfolds and kept moving around. That way the odour wouldn't have been pinned down, and a good part of the evening would have elapsed before anyone was able to point out the stinking culprit.

It would have been even better if everyone had shown up wearing those nose plugs like the girls wear in synchronized swimming, except they probably hadn't been invented then. But clothespins would have done the trick. And with both the blindfolds and the clothespins, we could have played a game called, "See no evil, smell no evil." The winner could have had my pants to take home.

Attempting to stand upwind of people all night, I didn't enjoy myself one bit. And neither did anyone who came within smelling distance of me. I didn't like the look Betty's father gave me when he passed by me. He took a big sniff and then scowled; if I hadn't felt so much love for his daughter I would have said, "Well, sir, I hope you don't think I just went to the toilet in my pants." Then I would have taken Murray's hand and left the party once and for all. But it's just as well I didn't since it might have broken Betty's heart. Better that her nose be broken so she couldn't smell me.

Murray and I were glad when the party broke up, because we were tired out from playing the part of handsome movie stars under such stinking circumstances. We headed for home and made a perfect landing over the mucky slurp of the dirty duck hole, just like the astronauts on the moon.

It was now nine-thirty and Pa was tucked safely in bed, resting up for work the next morning. It was time to start washing our pants in the antique washtub with P & G soap. The lustre that is noticeable on new pants was now gone, and our new pants began to look like sink rags. We changed the water many times, thinking they had to come white. While I was giving them a dousing for the twelfth time, Murray made a clothesline on the dark side of the neighbour's yard so Pa couldn't see them at rest. We thought of telling Ma to tell Pa that he should get rid of the old washer because it turned clothes black. And if that didn't work, we talked of suggesting to Ma that she get rid of Pa. Then we would marry Betty and Ma could come to live with us and take it easy for the rest of her life, as long as we could keep getting food on tick at the Co-op on Pa's bill. (Pa had excellent credit at the Co-op all his life. All we had to do was give his number, and if we said we'd have a Mercedes Benz, they'd charge it to Pa's number without question.)

Taking our pants off the clothesline the next day before Pa had arrived home, we found that our pants had shrunk eight inches on the legs and four inches around the waist. There'd be no more parties for a while. Anyway, who would ever again invite two skinny little hunks of stink? No, our night partying dreams had shrunk as much as our party apparel.

As usual, Ma came to our rescue. She put our duck muck pants away for a few weeks, then told Pa, "The twins are growing so fast, they've outgrown their new pants. I'll buy them a pair each for their birthday coming up. And besides, Teedy, the shortest in the house, can have Murray and Andy's pants for his birthday in May." And what could Pa do but agree with Ma, figuring he had fathered twin boys who would soon be the size of Giant MacAskill.

12

A Cutey On The Loose

Chances were slim in our day that we would find a girl we considered beautiful and shapely, especially when we voted many times on our own handsomeness and won by a majority. Most all the girls around home looked like Myrtle or her dog.

Evenings in the summer, the young fellows, along with a few two-timing husbands, would line both sides of the street in the lighter part of town, sizing up any females who were able to navigate their way along. It only took a minute for a male's eye to x-ray a body from toe to head, and I was one of those x-ray technicians.

If I had ever been lucky enough to catch me a girl not attached to a dog, I wouldn't have been able to take her home. I'd have had to stay out under the moon with her since I had no money to take her any place. If I had taken a girl to our place, Pa would have put her to bed for picking me up, and me to bed for bringing her home. But, unfortunately, strictly in different beds, and with more security men guarding the doors than Reagan had on his visit to Russia.

But I had an aunt who was a sweet lady. And she and her husband did a lot for me after Ma died. I stayed there from time to time, doing odd jobs and eating quite well. They had a lovely old home with one of the largest fireplaces I have ever seen— you could bake bread in it. It could hold a five-foot log, or Santa when he dropped down at Christmas.

The house was on a hill and seemed to be closer to the heavens because there were no trees like at home. Just to look out the window this evening would almost make a cow bark. The moon was full, just peeping over some light clouds. Luckily, the husband had a church meeting this night and my aunt was going to visit friends, so she said, "The house is yours for the evening, Andy." Zowie. Now all I needed was a female. Fortunately, everything was working in my favour because the night before I came upon a gorgeous creature in town, and she had agreed to meet me the next evening in town at seven o'clock. I would rather have met her in a field or half-way up a hydro pole, so I wouldn't have to pass all those peeking males hating my guts because I'd captured this beautiful stranger who'd only been in town two nights.

But this was to be my wedding night. With my relatives both gone, I made a cosy fire that would burn for hours. Other people roasted chestnuts, but my aunt had none, so my girl, when I got her, would have to settle for potatoes, and I would convince her they were better for her. I had worked all day making sure everything was immaculate. I had lugged in lots of wood and scrubbed the living room and the kitchen. Everything was shining, even me. I thought music might be welcome and would put me further into ecstasy, so I made for the radio, but with only one station I had to settle for a half-hour of stock quotations followed by the marine weather forecast.

Finally my lair was prepared and I was off to seize my prey. Down the main street I sauntered until I met up with my gorgeous creature. Filled with pride, I passed by all the staring males with my girl. Some of them had strange expressions on their faces, as if they were trying to tell me something. But all I could think of was, "Eat your heart out. I've got something here that's brand new— never been used."

Half-way home, her sweet, rounded mouth told me her name was Molly and that she was from Toronto. Thank God, I thought, because if she'd been from any part of the Atlantic provinces, ten to one Pa would either have had a fight with her grandfather, or spoken poorly of her mother. So I had no strikes against me yet, as far as Pa was concerned.

We reached our love nest and I flitted from place to place, checking the fire, the radio. The fire was red and sparky and I tried to get some romantic music. As I strolled from room to room, I knew she was eyeing my gait as I swept past her chair. "Will you have some tea?" I said shakily, as her big blue eyes looked into mine, which were almost closed, trying to look sexy.

I was getting weaker and weaker all the time because of what I had under my roof all to myself and so beautiful compared to what I had been visiting for the past few weeks; Teedy with a pit sock around his sore throat for two days, Murray going around with a salt pork poultice where he stuck a rusty nail in his foot, and Pa home from the pit with the croup.

At this age I used to sneak smokes, but Pa didn't know it or I would have been on trial for my life instead of here with this dish listening to the marine weather forecast for Anticosti and Banquereau. She swiftly smoked the first pack of tailor-mades I had ever owned, after I'd busted the seal. I was good at ripping packages open, mostly brought on by revenge for some punishment Pa had meted out.

I sat an antique tea-pot, soda crackers and little slivers of cheese on a small table in the centre of the room. Remembering that my aunt had set about eight small mouse traps a few days before, I almost told the young lady to eat as fast as she could so we wouldn't be invaded by mice.

Rather bashful, I sat nearly four feet from her throughout the evening, always waiting and watching to see what she was going to do, wondering if she was going to jump on me; not really scared, but on the alert in case Pa popped in, maybe after having heard from a jealous bunch of males in town that I had looked abducted.

I didn't have to coax her to take a cigarette. She was about five ahead of me, disintegrating them before my eyes. I believe she sucked in a whole cigarette in one puff. The package only held ten and cost fifteen cents, a day's pay. But I let on there were lots more where those came from, which was true if I went to the Co-operative, got them on credit, changed the bill to read two pounds of sugar, then placed it where Pa kept his receipts for the week. I should have shown her where I had changed it on the receipt and gotten her to take two tablespoons of brown sugar instead to cut down on her smoking, telling her it was much healthier for her, just like the potatoes.

One hour had passed and the only thing I could think of to talk about was picking coal on the shores for our fire in the winter. I could see I was tiring her with such sexy conversation, but I couldn't help it. Coal it was for the night and I couldn't stop talking about it unless Pa changed over to wood, and then I would have talked to her about wood, a much more exciting topic. The look on her face told me she'd turned against coal forever and would never burn it in her stove, even if she froze to death. And me, not quite forever, as we burnt it breakfast, dinner and supper. She took another cigarette as I reached for the feather-light package with only one left. Why, I'd never smoked that many in a whole month, when I scrounged up butts from the ball field and manufactured them into full cigarettes.

But I must admit she still looked sweet, even with a cigarette dangling out of the side of her mouth like Spider MaGoon. "Andy," she said in a low, husky voice like something from another world, "I should go now." Heavens, I was prepared to stay there forever, talking about coal, no matter how tired it made her. If she got that tired, I could always have put her to bed and just watched her, that's all.

I was trying to be a gentleman and not take advantage of her on the first date, but watch out the second date. It would be, "Bring your mother, gal. It'll take two just to control me. I've been reading up on women."

Helping her on with her blue coat with the fur collar, I was still in heaven knowing we would get cosier on our next date. The moon shone only on my sweetheart as I walked her back to town. The stars even huddled together to make the moon brighter for our romance. When we arrived at the lighted section of town, there were still plenty of males standing around watching us.

Strutting proudly like a bantie rooster, I reached for Molly's hand. The onlookers took on a look of horrified surprise as we passed by. You'd have thought I was walking hand in hand with a vampire. The guys didn't even look at her. Their eyes seemed to be full of fear for me, as if I was about to be guillotined. Ah, jealousy, what it does to a person. Suddenly, Molly said, "Oh my, watch it, Andy, that's my husband coming toward us."

Down the street bounded a six-footer who looked like he'd just escaped from the pen to find the interloper and squeeze him to death like an orange.

Here I'd been running around with a married woman in full view of the world and her husband, two-ton Tony. Just wait until Pa got wind of this, if I ever made it past Big Foot. To this day I'm not six feet tall, unless I stand on my car, so you can see why I didn't want to tangle with this man. In seconds, I unhooked Molly's arm from mine. Knowing the town much better than either of them, I took off, running behind buildings, out driveways and three times around the town's horse trough, until I came to the jewellery store of a friend of mine where until a few minutes ago I might have been going to look for a ring for Molly, to be paid for with gum wrappers.

Looking at my ashen face, my friend said, "You look scared, Andy. What's up?"

"Quick, hide me," I said. "There's a giant after me." I didn't stop to tell him I'd been running the roads with Mrs. Giant. Without any ado, he whisked me to the back of the shop and said, "Stay there until closing time and I'll get you then." Two hours is a long time to wait when you are stuffed in a muggy bathroom with nothing to read but a roll of toilet paper and the make of the toilet. At closing time, my friend sneaked me out the back door and drove me home to my brothers and Pa.

Pa had just retired for the night, and Billy, Teedy and Murray were waiting for me to give them a blow-by-blow description of the night's events. Apparently every second person in town knew I was running around with a married woman. I could see a little jealousy in their eyes. Then Billy broke the spell and said, "Even Pa knows about it."

But Pa wouldn't have to worry about me because they said her husband was renting a place near the school. So I guess it would be hookey again for a while, until I could persuade some plastic surgeon to reconstruct my face. (I could pay him off in coal.)

But what a wasted evening I had just put in. To think I fed my first pack of cigarettes to a married woman who didn't leave the mice a pinch of cheese. And to top it all off, she didn't even like coal. The clincher is I haven't seen a full moon since, unless I look in the mirror at where I just got my flu shot.

13

The Final Plunge

An argument with Pa one day erupted in a change of living. I packed my peck paper bag and went to stay for a while with my aunt and her husband. He was very awkward, like a bull in a china shop, in everything he undertook. He knew that everyone knew this about him, but he didn't much appreciate anyone saying anything about it, or his temper would flare.

On one of his good days, a bitter day in January, he pointed to a window that had been patched up for quite a while. Twenty below and storming, he declared out of a blue sky that he and I should put more putty on the patch. "Andy," he said, while I was waiting to hear a soap opera on the radio, "I don't like drafts. We can plug that in a few minutes."

Like a man who had a mission, as though he'd received a sign from God, and against his wife's ravings, he was determined to go on with the task, even if it killed him and the entire population of Cape Breton.

I pulled on three overcoats, one over the other, and grabbed a pair of discarded pit socks for mitts to face the arctic temperatures. Jutting out his chin like Kirk Douglas and throwing his wife a glance that said he'd go through hell or high snowbanks for her, surprised even her. With a few icy tools in our hands, we backed out and around, letting our backs take the brunt of the storm, like Nanooks of the North. I began rolling putty around a mile a minute in a cold hand. He applied little chunks of it to the faint draft like he was filling a tooth.

Inside the warm kitchen, his wife was still dazed at her husband's attempts to fix the window on a night like this, up to his hips in snow like Frosty the Snowman.

Plugging piece after piece of putty into the crack, he looked through the window at her with a cocky slant of his head, as if to say, "I've got more brains than you give me credit for." He was doing a good job. The storm was getting wilder and wilder as the wind howled a mournful warning. Finally he had the draft eliminated. Just at this stage of intense pride where he was almost bursting with his new exalted position, and just as he was about to rush in for his wife's praise, he stepped aside for an instant, threw up both hands in a clapping manner as if keeping himself warm, and threw another arrogant look through the window at his wife. Then without giving it a second thought, the stocky man turned around and leaned right up against the many-patched pane.

It didn't surprise his wife one iota when the glass shattered all over her newly waxed linoleum, like an eggshell dropped from the ceiling. Still flinging his arms around to warm his embarrassed body,. his expression was now something like that of a sad puppy dog and now read, "Accidents like this can happen to anybody." The triple-patched window was now disintegrated. I allowed one peek at his wife. She was shivering and stuttering, "W-h-a-t d-i-d I t-e-l-l y-a-a?"

He wanted to place the old coal stove against the opening to stop the icy breeze. Planning to keep the stove well-filled, he figured the wind, if it had any brains, would blow in the other direction as soon as it struck the red hot stove. He may have been the first man in history to ever try to burn the wind, and change its direction at the same time.

His wife came out of the bedroom dressed as though preparing for a three-day ski trip in the Alps, except she only went as far as the table to remove the food.

All we had to cover the window with was cardboard. Cutting it in the shape of the double frame, we now had to fit it into place. With the wind blowing like it was, I thought that if he could lie on two chairs with his feet holding the two corners of the pasteboard at the bottom while I hung from the ceiling, then I could hold the top corners with my spread feet. That would have worked magnificently if his wife could have pushed in hard with the palms of her hands against the centre of the pasteboard. At least we'd have had it under control for that moment, but there was no way for me to stay on the ceiling indefinitely, unless they nailed me there. Meanwhile, it was like trying to hold off a hurricane with a kleenex.

Finally, I grabbed two woollen blankets off the bed, folded them four ways to fit perfectly over the fixed and unfixed panes. Outside he and I went with the hammer and flat-headed tarpaper nails. I made sure to do the tacking, not trusting his clumsy hands around the surviving window. Once I hit him squarely on the finger while he was holding a nail on target for me. He never as much as said "ouch" when I missed the nail, but looked at me as if he'd had it coming to him and I knew he did. After tacking ten nails up, the blanket was taut and the wind had no place to blow in, so we retired to the gradually warming kitchen.

His wife was so relieved by the job that she had a half-smile on her face when we opened the door. Coming in first, I received the smile, knowing it wasn't meant for him. He stomped in quite happy, sporting a grin from ear to ear until his eyes met hers. His red nose and frosted moustache drooped as she displayed the same face he had looked at ever since the break.

There was another time I'll never forget. They were expecting company coming from another town. My aunt had been after her husband for two months to either get a new parlour table or fix the legs on their old one. The more dishes she put on it, the wobblier it got. He got some kind of instructions on how to fix it from a man who worked with him in the mine. I remember fixing one of the legs with him. It was hardwood and the holes were all too big for the screws. He pounded large spikes into the holes and after pressing down really hard on the table, said, "That guy really knew what he was talking about."

The big day came for the company to arrive. As usual, my aunt was well prepared with a large baked ham and all the trimmings. The table seated the six of us comfortably. After grace, everyone was in position for a really tasty meal. My uncle, at the head of the table as usual, was doing his best to show his best manners when my aunt reached for the salt, which was a little too far up the table for her. Her husband, always at her side in time of trouble, noticed the slight trouble she was having and said, "Here, I'll get it for you." And with that, he put his full weight of two hundred pounds on the crippled table leg. The whole table collapsed. And the way it slewed as it fell knocked most of us off our chairs, with hot vittles strewn all over our Sunday best. Some of us were laughing, but my aunt wasn't one. A full bowl of cranberry sauce had sprayed my uncle from the sleeve of his white shirt all the way down his back. He looked like he'd been run over by a train. Luckily my aunt's tea set was still on the buffet, or we all could have been like Casey Jones, scalded to death by the tea.

The large ham was saved just as it rolled off the platter. But the vegetables were ruined because all the bowls had broken when they hit the floor. Once the commotion had settled, we all retired to the square kitchen table where we had the ham and loaves of new bread and butter. As we sat round again, another small grace was said by my aunt, "Please Lord, if anyone needs the salt, let him get up and walk for it."

Finally, the long winter ended, spring rolled around and the old house seemed to breath a sigh of relief. The kitchen floor, ceiling and walls were immaculate, as were all the other rooms, from the thorough spring cleaning my aunt gave them. Mu uncle was just as clean. Having lived with her for forty years, he had to be.

One warm evening, after a great meal of fried pork chops, three vegetables and apple pie, with the day still young, she suggested that he and I take on the job of cleaning the outhouse, something long past due. His blue eyes brightened and a look of achievement came over him. With the little I knew, and the nothing he knew, we could tackle anything neither of us knew.

Her husband had a four-by-four foot hole for his waste, about five-feet deep, and over this was placed a wooden frame. It was on this frame the outhouse rested. When cleaning time came around, a new hole was dug as close to the old one as possible. Then the toilet was lifted and placed on the new hole, and the old one was covered in.

So Stan Laurel and Oliver Hardy proceeded to attempt this menial task, while a worried wife called out many times in her fast voice, warning to be careful. He would look at her in disgust, saying, "Keep still, woman." At the same time he was giving me a nod meaning, "Does she think I'm that stupid?" while in my mind, I'm saying, "Yes."

Doing all the digging myself to spare his health, I made sure the new hole was the same dimensions as the old one. About two feet from the old site new wooden sills were fitted on, then spiked together. A squeaky door opened, and a voice warned him once again, "Be careful." I grappled onto the most vulnerable place at the back of the building so I could watch his short steps. The first lift relieved the old rotten sills of their duties and they tumbled into the messy pit. A little to the left, then to the right. Everything was going well. With it half off its former resting place, we took a breather. I could see the important "How's that?" look on his face as though he had done it alone.

On our next lift, once again his pride got the better of him. He changed his position without telling me and shifted his grip to the centre. With almost all the weight on me, like Charles Atlas, I commenced to carry the whole outhouse toward the new hole. All at once he realized I held most of the weight. Ever so considerate, he rushed to grab the corner he had started with. Not able to see where he was going, he stepped too close to the hole, the sods gave way and, whoa, he was up to his navel in the centre of what looked like a mess of over-cooked spinach.

I dropped my end. Now I could get a look at my illustrious helper. Before I could do anything, the screen door flew open and a voice kept repeating, "Leave him there, leave him there!" But anyone would have helped a boa constrictor out of this scrape. Looking at the tears in his eyes, I felt genuine pity for him. But how to get this two-hundred pounder out? I only weighed one hundred and fifteen.

He was wearing knee-high rubber boots, which didn't help any. If I grabbed his hands, which he was holding over his chest, the weight of him might pull me in head-first and I'd be smothered. The only clean places to grab him were by the jaws or the ears.

What I needed was a crane. Then an idea came to me. I got three six-inch wide planks to make a platform across one side of the hole, and up he slithered like a seal on a clamper of ice, but not clean and shiny like one. Two rubber boots were missing when his feet entered the atmosphere and would be missing until the end of eternity as far as I was concerned.

I tried my best not to get too involved in the touching of him. The best spots were on his upper torso. I won't even mention the odour, but my heavens, we should have burnt him. Bewildered, he finally dragged his frame up off the platform so he wouldn't fall back in again. If that had happened, the only fair thing to do would have been to shoot him.

He sat there on the new grass like a bundle of liquid fertilizer. The upstairs window was flung open, and out in parachute fashion flew pants, shirt, drawers, the works, followed by a yell, "Don't come in the house." I grabbed the clothes and rushed to the coal shed out back of the house, which was kept as clean as a hospital.

What a refreshing scent, the smell of new coal and the wind letting summer's sweet breath waft in through the unfinished shingle boards. I hated to call him in to stink up these pleasant odours.

He couldn't get his clothes off without my help, so I took a deep breath, held it and made for him. No zippers in those days was an advantage. A zipper would not yield in this substance. Between the two of us, we yanked the stained pants sloppily from his bottom, like we were skinning a bear.

A long-handled shovel was used to transport the foul clothing to the discarded hole. The hardest job was relieving the hind pocket of his heavy pants of the billfold. Tubs of water and a hose were set up, and a thorough bath was in progress. We should have requested a herd of elephants from the circus that was in town to come to his house and give him a good hosing.

Allowing the hot sun to pour over his naked body, in no time he was shining like a Valley apple. And soon he was in clean clothes again, he rehearsed his opening speech before entering the house to confront his wife, knowing he'd had all he could stand this day. Surprisingly, nothing was said, so he went to his favourite chair and in a few minutes was fast asleep; a dream to look at now, compared to an hour before when he fell in. But at least he had been smart enough to keep his head above water, and years later could tell his grandchildren about the time he lived in a cesspool.

Adulthood

14

Grown Up, Again!

Well, here I am, all grown up again. In this section you will find me having trouble with my teeth and a crown that kept coming off. Well, since I wrote that piece, I've had even more trouble with my teeth.

I remember we were taught from infancy to keep our teeth clean, except by one toothless old hag who visited us occasionally. She said you could brush your teeth too much, I think because every time she came we were scouring our teeth and giving her our pearly grins. She hated us. We could tell by her toothless, unpearly grin. I knew she would have liked us to have a gaping hole of a smile, just like hers.

Well, now I've got it. I never thought I'd have to rely on false choppers, but as filling after filling fell out and appointments to fill up the cavities were hard to get, I began falling apart along with my teeth. So I thought I'd worry no more. I'd just get the eight teeth that were giving me all the trouble extracted. Now, don't get the idea I'm a brave, tough guy when it comes to teeth. No sir, I'm the cowardliest man known to a dentist chair. It's not just the dentist I'm scared of. It's everything in his office; if he were to bring in a goat while I was visiting, I'd believe it had come to extract my teeth with its horns.

At the dentist, he had me press down on a tasteless fungus he plugged into my mouth and a print of my teeth was made. He said, "I'll give you a call when the teeth are ready." I still had my top teeth. Three weeks later, I was outdoors when my wife called me in, saying, "You had a phone call. The dentist says your teeth are ready."

"Good," I thought, "he can put them in right over my old ones."

I just had to build up my courage to sit in his hot seat and lose my sexy smile and my gnashing ivories.

In the dentist's chair, with my accelerator to the floor, he yanked out all eight teeth, placing them in a kleenex like half-popped popcorn. He passed me the mirror. I looked like a newborn as I gave my first hideous laugh. Then he came at me with the new teeth and fitted them into my mouth. I was now the image of a little monkey with his top lip full of bananas.

The minute I pressed the false uppers to the live downers, I knew life would never be the same. I'd never be able to bite thread again, make wolf whistles, chew my fingernails or bite people. And whatever hopes I had of becoming a vampire were dashed. I'd probably leave my teeth in my victim's neck. It would cost a fortune to keep me in teeth. I was like a child taking its first step. I was sure if I swallowed, down would go the full set.

I had to avoid frivolous use of the letter T, as in turnips and third, and I more or less had to give up laughing because the compressed air caused my teeth to be blown right out of my mouth, like a dragon breathing fire.

So my advice to young people is take care of your teeth. Be careful what you bite and if a filling drops out, have it filled immediately, even if you have to go to a brick mason. He probably wouldn't charge much to trowel a speck of cement in the cavity. And then you'll wind up like our Uncle Joe, who in his eighty-fifth year never had a bit of trouble with falsies; when he gave that familiar old smile, everyone could tell he had his own teeth— the both of them.

I always have trouble with new cars, too. The last one I bought, I was quite proud showing it off, even though I was going deeply in the hole on the payments. Meeting a guy uptown, I knew he was jealous by the way he said, "What, a new car?" Trying not to be too much of a show-off, I said, "I've had it for weeks," as I preened and patted the hood. I went into the drugstore for a few minutes, came out, and knowing this guy and his friends were still watching me and my car, I walked swiftly up to it like I was in a big hurry, swept them an arrogant glance, said, "See ya," then opened the car door, slipped into the seat, and slammed the door behind me. I was in the back seat.

Do you think I jumped out or let on to them that I made a mistake? Not on your life. I waited for over an hour for them to leave, pretending I was leafing through some papers. I wouldn't have had to wait for them to leave had I been able to drive the car from the back seat, but maybe I'll take a course in that next year.

The last few years I've bought vans. Having bought a brand new one last summer, it was a lovely summer evening when Rhoda and I decided to take our first drive. Off we headed to a small canteen about six miles from our house. There must have been fifty or sixty people around, having pop and ice cream. Running in to get us some ice cream, I made my way back to the van with most of the people watching the shininess and newness of my vehicle. Upon reaching the van, Rhoda opened my door for me, then held the ice cream and pop, giving me a chance to close the door. Many eyes were looking on as I slammed my door quite hard, but it didn't close. Not only that, it wouldn't close no matter how many times I tried. People were still looking. Rhoda went into a laughing fit and said, "I'll get out my side and see how this door closes." So out she hopped, touched a few cogs here and there, jumped back in the van, went to give her door a slam, then said, "Now mine won't close, Andy." The car only had thirty-six miles on it, but neither door would close.

Well, I wasn't going to ask anybody at the canteen about it. I didn't want to give them a clue that the doors on my brand new van were jammed. Trying not to make too much of a spectacle of ourselves, after Rhoda calmed down from her hysterical laughter, we made our getaway.

So that our doors wouldn't look like Dumbo's ears flapping as we drove away, I had to hold my door shut, shift gears and drive, while Rhoda had a death grip on the door on her side.

Laughing crazily as we pulled in our yard, we gave the owner's manual a good going over and finally spotted the trouble. It required a screwdriver. Many times afterwards when one of us was rushing somewhere, our coat or shirt sleeve would trip the works, and the only thing that would remedy the cogs would be a screwdriver. Lord help you if you didn't have one, for you'd have to drive gripping your door and wishing you were handcuffed to it. Thank heavens there weren't two more doors in the back, or else we'd have had to lie on our back holding the front doors with our feet and the back doors with our hands, driving home that way. But we would have needed a periscope to see.

Then there was the time I was working in a grocery store for an elderly lady. She was peeling potatoes, turnips and apples for supper, so I got her to put all the peelings in a big brown paper bag. Next I waited for this little boy to come into the store. He was a quiet little fellow and willing to run small errands for me; I'd usually give him an ice cream or some chocolate milk. When he appeared, I asked him if he was scared of cats. He said, "No, I've got one home."

"Well," I said, holding the eight-pound bag of dead weight peelings about three feet in front of me, "This here is a wildcat." I could see his eyes widen on the word 'wild'. I continued, "I'll give you a big maple ice cream if you'll take the wildcat up to that house and let it out." He was all in favour and not the least bit excited as he finished his maple treat. After he had eaten the ice cream, I passed him the bag of peelings very cautiously, saying, "Now, don't let him out until you get in front of the house. Then you can put him down, but be careful, he might attack you."

The little fellow looked seriously at me and asked me if I had an old glove to carry the wildcat. I found one and passed it to him. From there on it was one of the funniest things I have ever seen. He never took his eyes off the bag as he picked it up very gingerly. He carried it with a death grip so carefully that it didn't even swung back and forth. He walked about a block to the house, sat the bag of peelings gently down without opening it and leaped back out of the way, waiting for the wildcat to appear. Five minutes went by. He moved up to the bag again, and then away he scooted again, as if he had heard it meow. This scampering back and forth went on for about a half an hour. At last, he went into the house and in a few minutes came back out with an old man who crept up on the bag of peelings with a shotgun, as if stalking a deer. The little guy was ten feet behind him on his belly. Suddenly, BLAM, there was a fifty-foot swirl of vegetable peelings flying through the air in all directions, with the old guy and the little kid still looking for the wildcat. Then they began to laugh.

Next time the little boy came into the store, I asked him to pass me an empty box that was close to him. He said, "No sir, you come get it yourself. There might be a cat in it."

And then there was the day I died. When I was about thirty, I was rushed to the hospital in Portsmouth, Virginia with a bleeding ulcer. For twenty-two days I was confined to my bed without food or drink—just intravenous. After a month, still very weak, I was allowed to sit up for first time. That was a treat. I could see more of the surroundings and would watch each morsel of intravenous drip quietly into my arm. I had always heard during my childhood that a quick death would be to inject air into a vein, so I was glad the nurses kept a close eye on me.

One Sunday afternoon my brother Teedy came to visit me. His stay was usually two or three hours. The conversation came up about watching the bottle drip. Teedy said, "You have a good eighth of a bottle left, but we'd better keep an eye on it. You don't want air in your veins when it empties or you'll die instantly."

"Oh," I said, "my Lord, the nurses must know all this or they shouldn't be here."

After that we talked for an hour about how I was getting one egg without salt or butter and how I liked it. Suddenly Teedy gave a high, jerky screech and shouted, "She's empty!" Well, I had never been dead or in another world before, but in seconds, while Teedy was out in the hall raving like a maniac for the nurse to come, I began to leave the planet.

I knew Teedy had to go about four doors down to the nurses' station to get help. While he was gone, it took the little strength I had left to take a peek at the bottle. That peek sent me travelling alone, floating above my bed, watching Teedy and the nurse.

Why couldn't I have stayed alive until Teedy brought her in to see if she could save me? But it was too late, too late. No use. My whole life was ebbing; my body, my limbs were useless. I could have jerked the tube out of the bottle, but then I would have been in a room full of air. So what was the choice?

Just to die. I began choking slowly. So this is the way you go. Everything was blurry.

The weak voices I heard were in a language I wasn't familiar with. I started to float out the door of the private room as a feeling of goodness washed over me. Just then, with me feeling so good, I felt a slap across my face which must have left a five-fingered mark on me, and I awakened just as the nurse's hand was going back up. "Andy, are you with me?" she called. I felt like saying, "Not just yet. I'm having wing trouble."

Finally, opening my eyes slowly, I looked at a frightened Teedy and whispered, "What did they do to me?" Teedy, really surprised I had lived as long as I did, let the nurse answer, thinking that I'd leave them again on another flying spree if he spoke too loudly. She told me she was going to give me a pill to straighten me out. From then on, I asked for a refill when the intravenous bottle was quarter empty. I wasn't taking any more chances because a person tires easily flying around in a small room.

Which brings us to bats. Statistics say Central Texas has the largest bat colony in the world. I don't believe a word of it. We have the largest bat colony right here in our house. They don't hibernate or fly south for the winter. They just fly from room to room in our house. When they run into me, they stick and feel like hot bubble gum.

The biggest fright I get from a bat is when I'm asleep and my wife hears one flying in and out of the bedroom. She hollers out as loud as she can, at any time of the night, "Andy, there's a bat in the room." Holler that at a person who is sound asleep and watch their reaction. I wake up thinking I'm a baseball umpire, saying 'yer out'. I find Rhoda all decked out with the bedclothes around her hair looking like the King of Punjab in his turban. "Get him, get him, he just went out," she cries as if she's talking about a burglar.

This is the old bull fighter's cue to reach out and grasp his cape–a bath towel–and then pull it open like an accordion and stand in the doorway until the little flying bull comes back. "Watch your hair, watch your hair!" shouts Rhoda, leading me to believe that I have hair. I gave up watching it forty years ago. There was nothing to watch.

As I'm writing this, the temperature outside is zero and a bat is flying around the kitchen. So if they planned on heading south, they missed their flight, and if they are hibernating, they're doing it in our house.

15

The Day Santa Threw Me Off The Roof

You have all heard of the theory that some people are accident prone while others are not. After reading this next story, you can decide for yourself if I'm one who is, if I'm just jinxed, or if instead, some voodoo tribe has put a curse on me.

It all happened a while ago, a few weeks before Christmas, when I decided I would trek into the woods and cut some hardwood for a nice cosy Christmassy fire in our wood stove. Coming upon a tree that was about fifty feet high and about a foot at the butt, enough to keep me in fuel for a month and a beaver for life, I began sawing away at it with my handsaw like I was in the lumberjack trade.

Paul Bunyan would never have forgotten to notch the tree on the back side like I did; here I was with the tree trunk nearly sawed through and the pulp saw caught like a bear in a trap. I grabbed my axe and began notching away at the tree, but it was too late. In seconds, the wind, or was it that voodoo tribe blowing on it, reeled the falling tree right across my chest and broke my ribs like they were peanut brittle.

Back at the house, Rhoda wanted me to lie down, but I told her if I did I'd never get up again. After all, it was only eleven a.m. Who went to bed at that hour of the day? (Pa had been dead for years.) I figured I could still do a few light jobs, like pluck feathers, beat eggs or blow bubbles. The garbage was light. I'd take that to the dump. But I wouldn't kick at it like that little fellow on T.V. who advertises Glad garbage bags. With my luck, I'd probably break my leg, even if there was nothing in the garbage but a bag full of froth.

Flurries were falling as I drove my car to the dump. Parking and getting out, I immediately came upon five or six

Javex bottles like I use for my dummy's heads. Next I spied a big box to put the jugs in; humming "Everything's Going My Way," I reached deep inside the box with both hands and was severely snared by three pieces of barbed wire. Probably the voodoo tribe was now sticking pins in their Andy doll's fingers. The more I tried to get my hands clear, the more the barbs penetrated. I was like a fish on a hook. I figured I would have to drive home holding the box of barbed wire on my lap to get Rhoda to help me clear. Or maybe I'd have to go around with that box on my hands forever, at least until I could travel to Haiti to find that bunch of voodoo guys who had it in for me.

Suddenly the barbs let go, and I ran to the car before something else happened to me. Who knows, the seagulls that were picking through the garbage might have all ganged up on me like in that Alfred Hitchcock movie. I grabbed a fistful of kleenex and sat there for a few minutes while my hands healed, looking suspiciously around in case there was someone or something waiting there in the dump to ambush me. Then I saw a guy I knew bringing an old chesterfield into the dump in the back of his truck. When he saw me there, he asked me if I wanted it for the Dummy Farm. "Sure," was my reply. He said he'd drop it off at my place in a while. That was great; I didn't even have to lift a finger, as if I could have if I wanted to. So I drove out of the dump toward home, steering with my lip and eye tooth.

Back home again, Rhoda looked at my hand hidden in a ball of kleenex and shook her head. After I told her what had happened, she covered my hands with iodine, powdered my face with sunshine and coaxed me to stay in the house for a while. It was one p.m. Who could stay in the house at one p.m.? Only the table and chairs. Glancing out the window, I said to Rhoda, "There's Tom, coming in with an old sofa for the dummies. He's going to drop it off out by the barn. If you can just give me a hand after, we can put it in the back shed out of the weather until summer." Rhoda said, "We'll get it under cover after you're better. Don't you lift an ounce. Look at the way you're walking, all stooped over like a chimpanzee, with your hands all cut to pieces like you've been squeezing ground glass." She didn't understand. It was only one p.m.

As Rhoda was fixing lunch, I was fixing to get that couch under cover right away, if I had to go out and hover over it like a mother hen over her chickens. When she saw me peering out the window, she said, "Don't even think of going out that door. The third thing that could happen to you might be worse than the others."

"Aw phifff," I said. "Don't be so superstitious." What did she think I was, accident prone?

My brain was working feverishly. I'd get that old sofa out of the weather if it broke my back. The only thing that might hold me back, besides my ribs, my hands, and Rhoda, was the winding, very zig zaggy tree-lined path that led to the shed.

Rhoda, thinking she had convinced me to rest quietly in the house, trotted up the lane to her sister's. She should have stayed home, tied me up and handcuffed me to the bed. As soon as she was out of sight, I sneaked out to the barn to get my wheelbarrow, as if I were planning a murder and that was what I was transporting the body in. Next, I attempted the feat of manoeuvring the sofa onto the wheelbarrow without lifting, bending, touching, smelling, breathing or blinking. Eventually, I had the large couch lying crosswise on the wheelbarrow like a beached whale. Then off I went with my long, wide load, with a red flag and a DANGER sign hanging off the seat of my pants, pushing toward the crooked trail through the trees to my shed, softly singing, "When you're down and out, lift up your head and shout, 'It's going to be a great day'."

The couch was blocking my vision as I came to a small hill that slowed my push. I gained a lot of momentum on the downward grade when all of a sudden, SPLAT. You could hardly believe the swift thrust of that chesterfield right into my face when I struck that tree. I was right in the middle of "Lift up your head and shout." All I can remember after that is hollering, "I'm shot," and waking up minutes later underneath the chesterfield, mumbling, "It's going to be a great day." I had run smack into a hardwood tree which threw the sofa at terrific speed right into my face, like someone had thrown a pie at me. There had been hunters around my property all day, so before I slipped to the ground in a daze I thought I had been shot, maybe by that voodoo bunch in Haiti. Rhoda was right, number three was the worst of all.

Later on in the house, with my face looking like a boxer who'd been really whipped, I vowed to Rhoda I would not be going outside any more that day, and that next morning I was going to be very careful of every move I made, probably not even using the toilet without her permission.

With my face swollen, my ribs sore and my hands almost helpless, I told Rhoda I would sleep on the outside of the bed, in case I had to get up during the night, to die under a mat in silence. And I could roll out onto the floor better than if I was behind her.

Next morning, Rhoda decided she'd get up and get breakfast. Hearing her rustle around like a mouse in a paper bag, I didn't bother to move my feet. I was lying on my side and my feet were resting one on top of the other. I thought, "Surely Rhoda will lift her weight over my feet." Just as these thoughts were moving through my mind, she sat down hard on both my feet. It wouldn't have been so bad if she had continued right on over me. But no, she just sat there for seconds like she was watching a movie. My foot bones were crushed, so I couldn't pull them out from under her and kick her out the window, as much as I would have loved to; with my smashed ribs, I couldn't holler for the police; with my useless hands, I couldn't smash at her or tear her hair out in fistfuls.

Nonchalantly, as if she hadn't almost severed my feet at the ankles, she stepped down onto the floor and off my crippled feet. She placed her two good feet on the floor, saying very innocently, "You just stay in bed today. You have to take it easy." I knew I could almost take anything that day after the full weight of her on my feet. That voodoo bunch must have hired Rhoda to finish what they started.

A few days after all this was Christmas Day and I was doing a very good job of healing. Things had been going well for me, jinxed or not. I had recently won a quilt at a Christmas raffle, the proceeds of which was going to the Highland View Hospital in Amherst, where I would soon need to go. We had just come back from our daughter's, where we had spent Christmas morning opening presents with her, her husband and our two grandsons, David and Michael, who had come home for Christmas from college in Halifax.

Everyone had that Christmas feeling and everything was hunky dory and coming up roses— for the moment. But unbeknownst to me, that voodoo pack was beating its drums and on the warpath again.

I was outdoors with Little Boy, my dog, and I could still hear the Christmas carols faintly echoing through the storm door. Turning my eyes to the roof, I could see a bit of snow that needed to be cleared off before we went back over to Dianne's for Christmas dinner. My thirty-foot aluminum ladder lay under a tree. Frozen lumps of ice and snow hampered me as I placed the ladder against the side of the house. With visions of sugar plums dancing through my head, I grabbed my shovel in one hand and climbed the twenty rungs, humming the "Little Drummer Boy." I tossed my shovel onto the roof like a javelin and continued my climb off the ladder. Humming the "Little Drummer Boy" on the roof seemed to be much easier. Must have been the altitude. I had never sung on a roof before, but at times I would sing right out loud like a fat opera singer. Finally, I completed my job and, still humming that tune, I edged my way toward the ladder on my hands and knees. Feeling around for the top rung with my feet and tongue, suddenly, right in the middle of my "rum pa pum pum," I felt the ladder leave me altogether. I was now hanging off the roof, clutching at some frozen humps just like in the movies where these two guys fight and one guy knocks the other guy off the cliff; where he clings to the edge for a while. I was that cliff hanger. This was serious business. I couldn't even remember the next line of the song. But it would probably come to me before I hit the ground. No time to holler for help. (The "Little Drummer Boy" had clogged up my vocal cords anyway.) Even Superman couldn't have flown fast enough to save me from this. I had to drop or fly. As I fell backwards through the air like an acrobat doing a backflip on a trampoline, a number of things went through my mind. My life didn't flash before me. I just kept wishing I had fallen forward so I could have picked the spot where I would land. A nice twelve-foot-deep pile of absorbent cotton would have been nice. There wasn't even any snow around, just frozen ground. Who needed this on Christmas day? The main thing on my mind on my way down was that I still hadn't made out my will. I tried a few quick flaps of my wings before I struck rock bottom, but no go. Not a flutter. Then KARPLOP, lights out! Good Night Irene!

Inside the house, Rhoda heard the clatter of the falling ladder and the plop of the falling Andy. When she ran outside, I was stretched out next to my ladder like we were having a short siesta together and didn't want to be disturbed. My eyes and mouth were wide open, my mouth, I suppose, because I was right in the middle of "on my drum." Rhoda thought I was dead. Even my ladder thought I was dead. Rhoda said I had half a grin on my face. Must have had something to do with the drummer boy, or the voodoo people were now trying to tickle me to death with a feather off one of my own hens. Little Boy was barking loudly and Rhoda was saying, "Andy, say something," and shaking me till my teeth rattled. Why did she want me to say something? What did she expect me to do, recite "T'was the Night Before Christmas"? I would rather have sung the rest of the "Little Drummer Boy" when I got my breath back.

My eyes twitched like Dracula's when he was coming to life in his coffin. I murmured, "What happened? Where am I? Is there a drummer boy here?" Rhoda helped me and my battered body into the house, where I began to freeze to death like I'd just been pulled out from under an ice cake in the Arctic Ocean. Every coat and blanket in sight were wrapped round and round me like a mummy. Rhoda should have left me outdoors on the ground, grinning. I wasn't the least bit cold there. Or she should have taken me to Egypt and put me inside a pyramid; but there again, I couldn't sing the "Little Drummer Boy" there. I didn't know one word of Egyptian.

Soon, Dianne and David came over, trying to warm me up. As cold as I was, they would have had to set fire to my clothes. Soon the ambulance arrived. My memory was nil. I didn't know it was Christmas or that I'd been opening gifts an hour before. The voodoo guys had finally done it, they had turned me into a zombie. To the hospital by ambulance, my blood pressure was roaring almost to the point where it was interfering with the gas pedal. I went through a siege of x-rays, was bandaged up, needled, and put to bed for the night, then told to stay awake all night long because of the concussion. All I had to occupy myself with was a comb. I didn't know how to play it and I didn't have much hair. But I had a beard, so to keep myself awake I combed it continuously all night long and sang new words to an old song, "That Silver 'Bearded' Daddy of Mine."

A few days later at home, many neighbours came to visit and to give their sympathy to my condition. I had a concussion, a broken finger and a chipped bone in my elbow, not to mention very lame fingers from all the clinging I had done, or all the mishaps that had gone before.

But it was when they asked me, "How do you feel?" that I'd get all choked up and could hardly keep myself from bursting out crying. Their pity on top of my own was just too much for me to take. And I began to feel like this little fellow years ago in Cape Breton. He had just gotten his first suit of clothes. And was he proud when he wore it! When a neighbour dropped in, his mother said, "Now Babe, my dear, put on your new suit and show Mrs. Roper how you look in it." He came out of his bedroom in it stiff as a poker and standing at attention. As the neighbour praised him up more and more you could see him getting red, like he had high blood pressure.

His mother said, "Now Babe, walk to the sink and back." By this time, the neighbour was almost eating him up with compliments and pats. Babe was getting redder and redder, like a baby filling his diaper.

Then his mother said, "Now turn around for Mrs. Roper and walk over to the sink." More praise from Mrs. Roper. By this time, Babe was blue-black in the face from being the centre of attention for so long. His head was becoming the colour of a bowling ball. Then another order from his mother. This was the last straw. He could take the good words and the limelight no longer. Babe let out a terrible screech like some horror movie, started crying hysterically and ran to his bedroom. I believe years later he became an actor.

So if you plan to come and visit me with all my accidental injuries, don't dare show me one bit of pity or praise unless you want to send me screeching and bawling to my bedroom, and then become an actor. Just give me hell for going up on the roof on Christmas Day and ruining everyone's Christmas.

Now that I think about it, I may have been allergic to the "Little Drummer Boy," having listened to it non-stop for the two months before in all the malls. Even the doctors knew the tune I was humming before the fall. I believe they said it showed up on my x-rays. Another thing, I think I can vaguely remember Santa on the roof with me that Christmas Day. And either he was on that voodoo people's payroll same as Rhoda, or he was allergic to the "Little Drummer Boy" too; that must have been why he threw me off the roof.

16

My First Will and Testament

How many of you are scared to make out your will, you cowards? Do you expect to live to be as old as Methuselah? I'll bet even Methuselah didn't have as much to leave as we do, and we're poor and not nearly as old as him. God help the rich, God save the Queen, and what is the capital of Iceland?

Last spring I purchased from a printing office a do-it-yourself will for fifty cents. Each night I thought guiltily of those papers, knowing they should have been filled out, because I could die at any moment. Not that I had a fatal disease (at least, not that I knew of), but who's to say I wouldn't be flattened by a falling tree or star, or that I wouldn't trip over a dummy and bash my head in on a rock (they can be malicious in the morning before they've had their tea), or, for that matter, perhaps it was to be my fate someday to just laugh myself to death while seated at the kitchen table eating sardines and toast. You know how funny they can be.

A moment of sadness came over me when I finally decided to get at the papers. I felt as though I'd been told that I had only weeks to live, and there was nothing to be happy about, no matter if my dummies had decided to take up a collection and send me on a trip to the South Seas for two months. A trip to the lawyer to finalize this was exactly the same feeling as going to the hearse, so I stayed away from him and continued taking my vitamins.

How in the name of heavens can you be of 'sound mind' to write down that your son or daughter can have your house after the time it took you to pay it off. Just when you're free from the payments, some nut tells you to sign it away when you don't have an ache nor a pain. That's what kills the person. They forfeit everything in their will, so what else is there to do but give up and die. A person should start all over again in a different country under an assumed name.

This bleak feeling passed and I was raring to go again until I found myself giving away the rest of my possessions with no remuneration. It was rough, especially for a Scotsman. And it reminded me of a bachelor cousin I had who, when he died, did take it with him. He had accumulated oodles of money over the years, so when he died suddenly, a small posse of relatives invaded his little house to see what they could find. All that was there on an old dusty table was a handleless cup stained with tea and a rusty spoon. Everybody gave him lots of credit for being able to take it with him, but we found out later his place had been broken into and robbed shortly after his death.

I almost wished for someone to come and rob me. Then I began thinking it should be Rhoda who went first and not me, because she knows practically nothing about where all my tools are. She has a fit just trying to find my small screwdriver. I can see her now, praying to the Lord to ask me where I put the new shovel. The Lord would have to arrange to have me sent back to earth to show her where it was, but then if I still have the same poor memory I did on earth, I'll probably forget to return to him again.

I then started hiding certain objects I wanted to keep for myself. A friend had given me a rare silver dollar a few days before. I wanted that really badly. No one but me was to get it under any circumstances. Then I figured it might be quite a shock to Saint Peter if when we met I showed him my silver dollar. (I don't mean present him with it as you might think. He can find his own.) I'd just show it to him, then walk right through the pearly gates past Peter, still clutching it in my right hand, hoping he wouldn't make a grab for it. It wouldn't look good to have to wrestle the saintly man to the ground.

Having survived the summer without being shot, stabbed, poisoned, kidnapped or stapled, I knew I was living on borrowed time and felt quite lucky not to have read my obituary in the newspaper. So Rhoda and I got together on it.

If I go before Rhoda, everything I own would go to her. If she goes first, everything she has would go to me. But I don't want it. She has nothing but some make-up, stopped watches without straps, a drawer full of single earrings, Bingo dobbers, 1462 dead 649 tickets, and a wardrobe of old clothes. There's no room in my closet now. Besides, I don't believe this far along in life I'd become a transvestite just to wear them.

If a calamity should erupt where we're both eliminated, then Dianne, our only child, comes into the picture; she had to complicate matters by having two sons who will be looking for their share, having never lifted a finger to help me hoard the loot. Of course, we won't show the grandsons the will for fear of assassination all around, or that we'd have to forfeit our pledge to them now and end up in the poorhouse before we've even died.

I really don't see how my daughter can take care of this business of wills unless I'm allowed a leave of absence to try and steer her in the right direction, because Dianne is stupid in business matters of this spooky nature; there's no way I want my stuff wasted. I had quite a time accumulating the mess in the first place. At this stage, I feel I'll just have to keep on living, like it or not. Also, I wonder if Dianne will share the same fondness for my large collection of bags, both paper and plastic. Who would have the heart to throw away those colourful plastic objects? I'd take a chance on my life (I hope I have my will completed by them) by running out in front of heavy traffic to capture one in the wind. And had they invented them when I was a young pack rat, I'd have had enough to supply a city supermarket for one year. Never mind that they are destroying the ozone layer. With that big hole in the ozone layer, it will be easier to be zapped into heaven when the time comes.

What will Dianne do with my eleven hundred ties? Her sons don't know what a tie is. Also, I have all kinds of tams and hats. My daughter and grandsons wouldn't even be seen out in their yard wearing the bonnets I own. I'll have to leave them to my dummies.

As I said before, there are a few things I'd like to take with me. In fact, I insist. Neither Dianne nor the grandsons will get my wheelbarrow. I've had this aluminum wheelbarrow for thirty-five years. It's terrifically easy to push, even loaded, either it or me. I could even pack a few other little things in it that I'd hate to leave behind. Now I'll admit, I might be the first to enter the Kingdom of Heaven in a wheelbarrow. But

I'm sure they would let me through after I told them how much it cost and how easy it was to push. They could dispense with my wings. If I'm anything like my hens, I'll probably have lice in all those feathers anyway. No, all I'd need to get around heaven would be a little kid to push me from place to place all day long, what you'd call rollin' round heaven all day. They might even be able to use my wheelbarrow up there. For instance, to deliver Mulrooney's shoes to him when he kicks the bucket, or for that matter, Imelda Marcos'.

The best move I ever made was that I just got rid of my one hundred hens. I knew each one personally, but now the worry of them is off my shoulders. If I had passed them along to Dianne or my grandsons, the hens would have followed right in my footsteps to the great beyond, because nobody would have remembered to feed them.

Another dreary feeling came over me. I felt like I was already dead (I began having smothering spells) and that I was allowed back for an hour or so to settle my estate. What would I ever do with my Dummy Farm? The dummies deserved a decent ceremony; cremation, with their ashes sprinkled over Cape Breton Island, where most of their characters materialized. But I would like to take a couple of my favourites with me, maybe one on each side. I would need a big tomb. Perhaps King Tut's would do if all of his stuff was moved out. But then if anybody dug me up years later, they might think I was Charlie McCarthy between Mortimer Snurd and his wife.

It was all just so unfair. There we were giving things away left and right. In fact, we had nothing left or right. And not one soul has given us a thing. But then I remembered the saw I borrowed from a friend; while I was using it, he died. I don't know whether I should keep it, mail it, wait until he comes for it, or give it to him when I see him. I guess it all comes out in the wash. On second thought, I could get Rhoda to give him his saw. Then again, I wouldn't want to overload her on her first trip. She would already be carrying my little screwdriver.

It really had me puzzled about what to do with the little things I'd hidden, taken care of and worshipped for years. I have a barn full of things that no one will be able to find, like axes, drills, ice cream sticks and plastic birds. I've put them in special places and while I'm living I just don't have time to tell everybody where they are. In fact, I don't know myself.

Then there's my new sit-on lawnmower. I don't know why I couldn't be buried sitting on that. But if not, I'll have to come back every four weeks at night to change the oil, because as far as Rhoda knows, the motor could run on Pepsi.

I have about fifty beautiful paintings an artist friend of mine left me when he died. What am I supposed to do with them, build my casket out of them?

Thoughts run through my mind. Imagine how hard it is to leave a new car you just got finished paying for, or socks you never wore. What happens when a person's clothes are in the cleaners? Do they send them to the dead letter office? And how easy it would be for the cleaners to pass out a size 50 coat to my bereaved when I only take a 38, or a tight pair of pants with a shiny seat which proves whoever owned them was lazy, as he was always sitting down.

I'm back to graciously donating things all around the family as though I'm presenting each with a different verse to say in a play. I never dreamed we owned so much. I have boxes and boxes filled with bent nails and the worse part is, with the price of nails today, I love them. Then there's the carton of wooden ice cream spoons from when I used to sell ice cream. Who, sound mind or not, could part with those? And there are so many other small personal things I cherish and I'll really have to take with me if I have to sew little pockets all up and down my suit.

And what about my two geese? I guess I could hold one under each arm. But instead of heaven, I might end up at the top of Jack's beanstalk, with the giant after my geese.

I'd also need some aspirins. It's been known that headaches turn up after minor tremors in the bowels of the earth. I'd have to make sure I got an old-fashioned bottle of aspirins, because with those new-fangled ones where you follow the arrow, I could die again in seconds just trying to open them and I'd have to follow the arrow right to the doctors, if there are any in heaven.

Now, to cut down on your will, it's a good idea to be kind to your neighbours while you're still here on earth. For instance, if for three days in a row you've been feeling lousy, go to your friend and say, "Listen, brother, I have a Lincoln Continental. And tomorrow if I feel like I do today, it's yours." This way you are being kind and smart at the same time. That car is a long name to be written up in your will and besides, it's beginning to burn oil. Don't forget to tell them, "Use it with care, though, because I have ways of coming back." I figure if I can go in my wheelbarrow, I can come back in it too.

With all these things in mind, you can see why a person shouldn't die too hard, just lightly, so he can come back and get things running smoothly.

I can really identify with the Indians who took their hatchets and knives with them to the Happy Hunting Ground. I could take everything I wanted with me then, even if it meant building an ark; once there I could do a heap of bartering with the Indians. I've always loved a good swap. However, with my accumulation of goodies, they'd have to dig a grave for me the size of the Grand Canyon. If someone were to dig me up, the abundance of artifacts they'd find around my body would lead them to believe they'd discovered the Lost Continent of Atlantis.

And I mustn't forget to take a big box of toothpicks. I've been chewing on them continuously since I quit smoking, and I wouldn't want to have to start smoking again up in heaven. Wouldn't matter in the other place. Everybody smokes there anyway.

I've been thinking seriously about it all and you're a fool if you don't get really friendly with me before I pass on. I could will you some rubber tires encircling my trees, stacks and stacks of old newspapers, and a tiny pair of scissors I use to cut the hair out of my nose. And I know for sure that Rhoda has two million little pieces of soap lying around, and scads of old, old, old *Enquirer* magazines, plus a drawer full of pretty shaped empty perfume bottles, used vitamin containers and about 200 different-sized pieces of cotton batting.

And do you know what? I haven't got my will made out yet. I've decided not to go.

17

The Storekeeper

In 1940 I was honourably discharged from active service because of stomach ulcers. So, with a long list of what I couldn't eat and a much smaller list of what I could eat for my stomach trouble, I left Camp Hill Hospital in Halifax and arrived in Amherst, Nova Scotia.

I carried all my belongings in a paper bag; soiled socks, underwear, a wrinkled army shirt, a month's pay ($39), and my lists. Soup was number one on the list. So entering a squarely-built, unpainted grocery store, my eyes met the owner— an elderly lady with a limp and a sincere smile on her wrinkled face.

She asked me what I wanted. "One can of tomato soup and a package of soda crackers, please," I said as I handed her twenty-five cents. Looking at the cold can of soup and the package of crackers, the motherly look I kept getting made me ask the storekeeper if she'd warm the soup for me. "Come inside, dear," she said as she led me back toward the kitchen and heated my soup. As I was eating, darkness was approaching, so I said, "I have no place to go. Are there any cheap hotels here?" She'd already refused my twenty-five cents for the soup and crackers, and she said, "Don't worry, dear. I have plenty of room here and you are welcome to stay."

That first night, I enjoyed the most relaxing sleep I'd had in months. After a day or so, I didn't want to bum off her any longer, so I said, "Well, Mrs. White, I guess I'll go and find a job." But she wouldn't have any of it, saying, "You're not leaving this house. You're too sick to go any place. You can help me in the store. It's light work. I can pay you four dollars a week. And I'll get you better."

Happily I accepted; and as the days rolled by and I got to know her, I found her to be the most humorous, honest and hard-working lady I had ever known. She was scared of no one, and though the townspeople thought she was illiterate, in reality she was as smart as any lawyer when it came to her rights as a citizen, as they were to find out.

She took me under her wing like a wounded chicken and was very protective of me. If anyone talked badly of me in her presence, they had to put up with the consequences. She would hit them with whatever was closest to her.

She was a Roman Catholic and I was a Presbyterian. This started quite a chatter in the small town. "Why does she have a Protestant working for her and her such a good Catholic?" This talk just did more to fan the flames of humour between us. Each time we sat down for a meal, I would look in her direction and very slowly and deliberately cross myself in a very solemn manner. She'd burst out laughing. She loved fun and laughter and we had plenty.

She was soon relying on me to order what we needed in the store; bran flakes, canned beets, sugar and other items. Many times she said, "God sent you here," and she was beginning to look rested.

An ice cream company loaned her an ice cream cabinet, far from new and barely workable, which was supposed to hold nothing else but the company's ice cream. Mrs. White never listened to this. She put everything in there. She also had an old, motorless Coke box for pop and milk, which she got daily from a local farmer. This Coke box got its coolness from three buckets of water we'd throw in it at the start of each day. On warm days we had to change the water three or four times. The milk we used was raw, not pasteurized like today, and it soured much faster on warm days. But Mrs. White taught me the secret of putting two heaping teaspoonsful of Cow Brand Baking Soda into each bottle and shaking vigorously. With her combination German/French/Scottish accent, she'd speak up, "Dat will fix it." And of all the milk I sold for her, I never heard any squawks about it, except for a few customers who said that every time they drank Mrs. White's milk, they burped a lot.

She didn't buy in abundance like stores do today, just a dozen cans of beans or a dozen soap. And many times she'd run out before the weekly order man came again. One thing she always bought by the case was corn flakes— forty boxes— which she sold for ten cents each. Placing these articles on the shelf was my job. I always wished she had less space and more groceries. However, once I opened that case of corn flakes, I felt good. I'd line them up side by side on three shelves that ran for fourteen feet. With those cereal packages standing side by side like an army on the march, it took away that empty look. Why, I saw Mrs. White, once the boxes had been arranged, refuse a customer a box of corn flakes, saying, "No dear, it will only mess up my shelf. Wait till Tuesday." And I went along one hundred percent.

In the back shed was a fifty-pound slab of salt cod that had gotten too close to an oil can. Mrs. White was bound she wasn't taking the loss. So the fish was recommended to a few customers who had colds and sniffles, as they whispered and coughed, "I'll take two pounds please." A winter epidemic of flu that year helped us get rid of the oily fish. She told everybody it was cod liver oil, and we did a better business than the drugstore.

Then came a law that forbade selling on Sunday. When I asked her if she was closing, her answer was, "No sir, dere not stopping me," and we continued as usual. On Monday, we were confronted with a summons to appear in court at ten a.m. Didn't set her back one bit. Just kindled the fire of what she thought of the police and councillors.

I was to be her representative in court. She bulged me out with bills and away I went like Perry Mason, with enough cash to get Al Capone out on bail. Once at the courthouse, I met the evidence— a customer, and the judge would present a can of beans and a loaf of bread. "Guilty," was my cry. The first offence cost $5.50— a spit in the Atlantic to Mrs. White. At first I thought this would teach her a lesson, but she'd made that much just on the fish.

"Yes, sir. I'm staying open Sundays." Monday, another summons. I always represented her and was getting to know the judge and police quite well. "Guilty," again was my plea, as I spied the pack of cigarettes and a can of corn on the stand. Second fine, $10.50. Back at the store, "Pffff, is dat all? I'm staying open." She sold everything on Sundays, right down to the corn flakes, even though it upset their arrangement on the shelves. Monday, a rap, a summons, a trip for me again to the courts. A package of cheese and a bar of soap were the culprits this time. Same plea, "Guilty," $15.50, another drop in the bucket for Mrs. White.

Nothing was going to change her mind. And that was okay, because that was the last fine she paid. Don't think she closed. I figure the judge had no shelves for the groceries the police had seized and had to call it quits, or start a grocery store.

Since this was during the war, there were all kinds of important papers sent by the government for storekeepers to fill in concerning what they could and couldn't buy. Mrs. White's papers went as far as the old coal stove in the kitchen.

Liquor was rationed, a quart a month per person. This made it rough on the 1,500 soldiers stationed in the barracks two blocks from Mrs. White's store. Seventy-five percent of them passed her store every day. I had been in these same barracks so they were sure to come in to see me.

If the authorities caught you selling more than one case of pure lemon at a time, they treated you the same as if you were caught selling liquor. The fine for a first offence was two hundred dollars. The little bottles of lemon sold for twenty-five cents, and two kept a person quite giddy for hours. At dances, they were easy to conceal, though the odd blond or brunette compared your breath to a fruit cake.

Mrs. White found a man who would deliver all the lemon we wanted, with the cases done up in newspapers. The police got wind that our store was selling lemon to soldiers by the case. It was legal to sell them just one bottle, but only if they said their wife was baking a cake. The majority of their wives were hundreds of miles away and I knew it; although I felt one hundred percent better when they said those few words as I handed them their case to make a big, big cake.

Feeling a bit uneasy one Friday, I moved ten boxes of lemon and hid them from view behind a layer of candy boxes stacked three feet high. One of the oldest soldiers in the contingent, the toughest and the nicest, was a strong, well-built guy from P.E.I. He didn't give a damn for anybody, and if he left the barracks at five p.m., five minutes later he was high.

The bell on the store door shook madly this Friday, and three police entered. They caught me sitting on the counter, talking over army yarns with this drunken soldier. As the police entered like they were raiding the mob, one made straight for the kitchen, and another followed behind him, heading upstairs.

Mrs. White began fighting with the policeman who was searching her kitchen and nearly pushed him outside. He was somewhat scared of her, but continued his lemon hunt. The policeman who had been upstairs rooting around came down and asked me if we had any lemon. I told him we just had one case, and I almost thrust it in his face so he'd steer clear of the candy boxes hiding the ten cases.

Pointing at the illegal spot, he said, "What's in those boxes?"

"Candy bars, sir," I said, being used to calling Pa 'Sir'. He rerouted his course. He was also a bit scared of Mrs. White, as he could hear a free-for-all tongue lashing going on in the kitchen. At one point, he went into the kitchen to defend his partner just as my drunken soldier friend, with a big smile on his face, hollered out, "Give me three bottles of lemon." I said, "Are you out of your mind? Can't you see we're crawling with police?"

He had just heard the police asking if we had any illegal cases of lemon, but he kept getting louder and louder. He wouldn't shut up and said, "Hell, those guys have been after me since I was ten years old." Quickly I bent down, grabbed three bottles and cupped them in his hand. He staggered out, laughing away.

Just minutes later, the policemen could take no more of Mrs. White's brow-beating and stumbled out to the police car before she went after them with her mop.

We did so well with the boot-legged lemon, we thought we'd go into the meat business.

18

You'll Get No Meat Here, M'Dear

The only meat Mrs. White sold was bologna, because it kept unrefrigerated. But we used to have calls all the time from special customers for real meat. One lady in particular, a Mrs. Smith, had a dozen boarders and many times would say to Mrs. White, "Why don't you get some meat in? You could sell a lot here, especially on Sundays." Mrs. White had great respect and a real fondness for Mrs. Smith and would have tried to bring in hippopotamus hocks if she had requested them.

Next day, an elderly farmer came in selling potatoes. Mrs. White got two bags, and then steered the conversation around to beef. "Sure," said the farmer, "I can get you a nice side of beef at a reduced price." After thinking it over for a few minutes, a big smile came over Mrs. White's face and two dollar signs rang up in her eyes. Then she looked towards me and we both looked toward the ice cream freezer.

"Dere's no money in ice cream. Da cones took a jump," she said in her German/French/Scottish accent. Besides, she knew I hadn't learned the knack for scooping out the ice cream. I was noted for giving big scoops the size of grapefruit, while hers were the size of ping pong balls, except for Mrs. Smith's, and she would let me scoop for her. Mrs. White was embarrassed to have to keep telling me not to give such big scoops. So this was the answer to our problems, a chance to quit worrying about scooping and try our hand at butchering.

"Bring it by Friday," she told the man. "We'll have the ice cream sold by then." After this, she made my scoops look small beside the ones she was serving. To get rid of the ice cream, hers were top heavy and falling off the cone, and looked like she had sculpted Dolly Parton's bust on each side. Mrs. White kept telling me we would really make a fortune, because on Sundays you couldn't get a piece of meat anywhere unless you shot it back in the woods.

On Friday morning, the side of beef arrived. "How much is dat?" said Mrs. White, as she reached for an old black purse that probably held a thousand dollars. Ripping bills off from her roll like they were romaine lettuce leaves for a salad, she handed two twentiesto the short little man who was carrying the side of beef in front of him. The farmer's last words as he short-legged it towards his wagon were, "That's a fine beef you've got there." We didn't know it then, but it was too bad it hadn't stayed on the cow.

The afternoon was taken up looking for a suitable knife for the butcher; I was the butcher, having had lots of experience watching the cow on the baking soda box that the old lady added to the sour milk. If you looked at the cow real close, you could see it wag its tail, as if to say, "This is a store-keeper's secret."

I would have preferred a machete to do my slashing with, but settled for a razor-sharp knife. Making deep incisions in the beef, it's a wonder I didn't cut off both my arms as I scored, gashed, slit and sliced off every place I could see meat. I almost went at the cat, but he had too much fur.

Mrs. White had locked the store, even though we were right in the middle of business hours. She would brook no interruptions until after I finished the carving. She thought I was a genius, and relied on me one hundred percent, so she had me not only doing the cutting but also naming the cuts. There were piles upon piles of chunks all over the place, with Mrs. White moving them around to the different sections of the freezer like she was playing checkers. The back part of the store looked like a Chicago slaughter house. Everywhere you looked were huge bones almost defleshed, with haggily pieces that looked like they'd been chewed up by a chain saw.

The bones were easily named, hearing the double word so often— soup bones. Then I had to name the rest of the cuts. The bigger the piece of meat, the prettier the name and the more expensive. It was amazing, but it seemed that all this side of beef was T-bone and sirloin. When I cut off a large chunk of beef, it didn't matter if I sliced it off the cow's jaw, no doubt about it, it was either T-bone or sirloin.

Mrs. White had so much confidence in my butchery you would have thought I was Jack the Ripper. She'd hold up a raggedy piece that looked like a worn out maroon mitten and say, "What's dat?" Even if it was the cow's ears, I'd speak up, using her dialect, and say, "Dat's sirloin."

The sirloin was put in one heap, and believe me when I say it was a large heap, only surpassed by the T-bone heap. If she showed me some meat that had even a sliver of bone, though it be the cow's tooth, I'd say, "Dat's T-bone." Oddly enough, she never once picked up a piece of meat that I would call stew meat or round. Those were poor mans' cuts. We were only selling the wealthy cuts with our gigantic supply of T-bone and sirloin. I must have been the only butcher alive who could shear a slice off the cow's ankle and, after struggling with it for a while, turn it into a delectable T-bone.

Two hours had passed and the big surprise for our customers was almost ready. The ice cream cabinet would soon be giving birth to all the prime cuts of beef. Meat was stacked from the bottom of the freezer and pressed hard against the underside of the four covers, threatening to burst through like rising yeast. I pressed down hard on the lids, and then proudly rubbed my hands together at a job well done. I felt that I had mastered butchering much faster than I had learned to tie my shoes. Almost too fast.

The door was still locked. But there was considerable thumping going on, with people knocking and peeking in windows; with all the blood and gore around, they may have thought I slaughtered Mrs. White and put her in the freezer. But Mrs. White was just not ready to receive the public yet. Things had to be perfect for us, the cattle barons of Amherst. Out from a closet in the back of the store she came with a bulletin board. Cleaning it off with her apron, she said, "You have to advertise da meat. Nobody knows we have it but Miz Smitt," as she passed me some chalk. We would soon be rolling in gravy and mooing all the way to the bank.

I can still see how, with a flourish equal to Ed Norton's on the "Honeymooners," I marked down 'T-bone— 40 cents a pound'; then following that, in blazing chalk, 'sirloin steak— 35 cents a pound'. I didn't want to mess up the sign with round steak and stew meat. I even had Mrs. White convinced there was no stew meat or round on the side of beef that we had bought— that it was all on the other half of the cow. Then, in very small print, hoping no one would be able to decipher it unless they'd brought along a magnifying glass, I printed 'soup bones', which, if I'm not mistaken, included one of the cow's hooves, part of its skull close to the neck bone, its top set of teeth, and an old bone the dog had dug up in the back yard the day before.

The first customer who came in after Mrs. White opened the door was a loud, nosey woman that the old lady never could get along with. Just minutes inside, she started blasting Mrs. White for having the store closed. Then she spied the meat menu, saying, "Well, well, even meat now, what next? Give me a couple of pounds of that T-bone." Just as I was about to go in the back for the meat, I was nearly tackled by Mrs. White as she hung onto my sleeve, saying, "Da meat won't be ready until tomorrow."

"Humph, this is quite a store," said Mrs. Loudmouth, looking daggers at the old lady as she headed for the door, groceryless and meatless. As soon as she left, Mrs. White said, "Don't sell dat ting any at all. We may run short. We'll just keep it for our good customers like Miz Smitt."

Saturday rolled around, but strict orders came from the old lady, "We'll wait for Sunday. Miz Smitt will buy a lot of it den. And she'll be proud to be our first meat customer."

"O.K. with me," I said as I reached up and took the sign down until Sunday, humming "We're in the money."

Rising earlier than usual on Sunday to get the store in immaculate shape so the proud meat peddlers could make a killing selling their beef, I hung up the sign. After the sales we were going to make, Mrs. White would be able to buy a whole prize herd of her own, plus the pasture.

Soon Mrs. Smith appeared on the scene, smiling happily when her eyes focused on the meat sign. And I can still see Mrs. White's joyful look (like she was welcoming Mrs. Smith into the Kingdom of Heaven), as she placed her palm sideways flat down on the counter; looking directly into Mrs. Smith's face, just inches from her, she said, "Yes, Miz Smitt? What can I do for you today?" knowing that the meat sign told Mrs. Smith everything she wanted to know about meat, but was afraid to ask. "That's good," said Mrs. Smith, looking at the sign again. "You should sell lots of meat here. I'll take five pounds of sirloin, please."

Mrs. White, without moving from her position, except to take one hand and dramatically throw back a wisp of grey hair that had fallen over her eye, glanced in my direction and relayed the same request that I had heard in the first place. "Miz Smitt would like five pounds of sirloin." Wow, our first big sale. We should have had a bottle of champagne to christen the meat with.

I could have started from either of the two back compartments, as they contained nothing but sirloin. Reaching in the freezer to yank out some meat, my heart almost stopped. To get any meat out of that fridge would have been the same as trying to pick a piece of lava off another piece of lava after it had hardened.

Luckily, out in the front part of the store, Mrs. White was talking a mile a minute, telling Mrs. Smith the news of the week. She'll soon be getting some news from the weak, me. I was hoping her stories would go on into eternity, because that's how long it was going to take me to scrape, tear, chisel or tweeze off five pounds of sirloin steak.

I did make it look good, though, by striding to the kitchen and getting the table knife, but it was as useless as using a toothpick for a crutch. What I needed was a hand grenade from one of our soldiers, or a front-end loader to pick up the cabinet and deliver the whole thing, covers and all, to Mrs. Smith, to tell her to chip away at it for a while.

I could see Mrs. Smith was getting impatient. The old lady's yarns were coming to an end and she was sort of ad-libbing now. I wished she would break into a sad hymn of about forty-three verses. By now twenty minutes had elapsed and Mrs. White well knew that I should have had the steak weighed and wrapped, and that Mrs. Smith should have been getting a smile and some change and been on her way out.

When Mrs. Smith turned and walked to the other side of the store to pick up some other groceries, Mrs. White left her and came to my rescue to see what the hold-up was. She was not able to see my head, because by then I had it most of the way in under the front cover of the ice box, using the useless table knife to plane off pieces of meat the size of toenails.

As I turned my head, I almost screeched with laughter when I saw the old lady's grizzled head and bespeckled eyes peering directly into mine from inside the ice box, and whispering from the other hole, "Will I get da poker?"

"Yes, bring anything," was my defeated, frosty reply. I was embarrassed and I didn't want to come up. Maybe Mrs. White would do the kindly thing and just bury me here.

I knew Mrs. White would not let herself be seen by Mrs. Smith as she carried the dirty coal poker to my assistance to pry at Mrs. Smith's sirloin. Had I been a leprechaun, I could have gotten completely inside and given it a good pry with a round-mouthed shovel. As it was, I would need a laser gun, a power saw and a jackhammer all at once. Even chunking at the meat with the poker, and Mrs. White chattering at Mrs. Smith like a squirrel on amphetamines, I just couldn't stay under there any longer without earmuffs and a snorkel. I appeared into the atmosphere and hollered loudly and disgustedly, "I give up. The meat is all frozen together. It's impossible to chip off a spoonful."

Mrs. Smith said, "Well, I can come back in the morning," as the old lady sorried herself, saying, "O.K. Miz Smitt, come back tomorrow." Had she told her to come back in a week, it would have been more like it. It took five days of prying and digging before we got even enough for the two of us. We unplugged the freezer and removed all the lids, trying to thaw out the mountain of meat that looked like one big, swollen hamburg.

Mrs. White and I waited for the thaw so that we could replace the meat with ice cream, which wasn't that hard to serve to the customers. A friend of Mrs. White's gave her a recipe for mincemeat, but having it three times a day for a month made me feel I never want to see mincemeat again, even when made from choice T-bone.

Once we had finally gotten the cabinet all cleaned of meat, there was still a half-inch of steak on the bottom that we couldn't get out no matter how hard we tried. It was frozen right into the metal. And many times customers would tell us that our ice cream had a different taste than the store further up the road. They'd go on to tell us that they could not only taste the cream of the cow but the taste of the cow itself.

19

Don't Ever Trust a Bird

All my life I have loved birds of all kinds and descriptions. In my other books you may remember that pigeons were always close to my heart, along with hens. I was nuts about hens, and at one point considered marriage to a hen if Pa had given his consent. So you can see, I wasn't a mean person when it came to birds. That is, until I met up with the fiendish finch.

Many years ago I worked in a big department store, and in this store, along with all the other odds and ends they carried, they sold canaries, budgies, and African finches— black, robin-sized birds with two-inch beaks.

One day two good-looking girls were in the store to buy a finch and I was their salesman. Flinging back my shoulders and throwing out my chest, I displayed my most handsome smile, at the same time straightening my tie. You would have thought they were there to buy me.

When they noticed what a commotion the bird was making, squawking and leaping all over its cage like it was sitting on hot coals, they cautioned, "Don't pick him out with your bare hand. He'll eat your thumb." That was all I needed to hear. I'd show those beauties a thing or two about what the 'birdman' could do. Even though the boss had warned me many times to always wear gloves while getting the finches out, what care I for thumbs? Flashing my pearly whites and giving a devil-may-care "Tut tut, now don't you worry" nod of my head, I thought I'd impress those lovely girls by sticking in my ungloved pinkies. Why, if the cage had been larger, to show them how brave and manly I was, I would have crawled inside with Ferdinand the Finch and had a birdseed breakfast with him.

The girls were speechless with amazement at the courage their salesman displayed. Their eyes opened wide as I jauntily opened the door of the cage and proudly reached in as if I was going to bring forth the Hope Diamond. Then with an arrogant tilt to my head, I made a grasp for the finch. But with just as arrogant a tilt to his head, the foul finch locked his lengthy bill onto my forefinger like a robin latching onto a morning worm. I picked him ever so gently (like I was capturing a bubble) off his perch and pretended my finger didn't hurt a bit, and that this particular finch and I always had a rollicking, raucous racket together. And that we liked it.

I still hadn't gotten him out of his cage. Smiling broadly while he was snapping and biting at me, the girls were now holding their hands over their mouths, each sighing "Ah" with a quick intake of breath. At this moment, the bottom of the finch's beak penetrated under my fingernail. It was caught and so was I. Before I began to pull my finger out, bird and all, I sneaked a peak at the girls. Some changes had taken place in them. They were now blood red with laughter. Quite an impression I was making on them, Colgate smile, straightened tie and all. Bursting with laughter like that, they weren't pretty any more. They were too red. Forgetting all about my macho image, I dragged the bird out of the cage by its neck. It let out such a squawk its bill let go, I let go, and away it flew. I grabbed for the net we kept next to the cages and made a swish at it. I netted one of the girl's purses and an ashtray, which dumped an array of butts and ashes into the tropical fish tank.

After about fifteen minutes, thinking I might have done a better job with a fly swatter, I at last slapped him down into an empty fish aquarium, wishing it had been full of water so that he might have drowned. He would have been a lot easier to wrap for the girls. I could have put him between two sponges and they could have had fried finch for supper.

Meanwhile, these two girls were still laughing and almost in hysterics at my plight, and me keeping such a stiff upper lip. I had the bird still in my hand while I was opening the cash register to make my sale. I felt like slamming the drawer on him and leaving him there. One girl volunteered to hold him while I was ringing him in. I almost wrestled her to the floor, saying, "Are you crazy? I know those finches. You can't mess with them. They're out for blood." Then trying to slide back into my good guy image again, I looked toward the girls with a sweet smile on my face as if I was ever so relaxed and content, but the look I secretly saved for the bird was a hateful sneer of "I'll get you, buddy." In my heart I wanted to slap him silly and knock him over his shiny little head with a mall, maybe even the Edmonton Mall, but it hadn't yet been built. With the beaklock the dear feathered creature had on my finger again, I would have loved to take him to the kitchen section to whip him up in a blender and then sat on him.

Remarking how brave I was, but still snickering a bit when I wasn't looking, the two girls waited for me to put the fighting finch in a special box I wished was his coffin, so they could carry him away. (And, I hoped, bury him.)

Still clutching him, the bird made another snap at my fingers like an enraged clothespin. When he finally released his grip this time, not wanting to lose face with the girls, I poised him just inches from my mouth, looked in his beady eyes, and scolded him as you would a playful puppy. What a mistake that was! Old fuzzy finch didn't like that a bit. Reaching out with the thrust of a hot-tempered gander, he almost tore the bottom lip off my face. I didn't like that a bit. I had an awful urge to bite him, but he probably would have torn out my tongue. My eyes watered; tears of joy. I still had a good hold on him like he was a large Clydesdale I had to keep in line. But I made sure he was far from my face— almost into the next state. I would have liked to wring him like a mop. I not only should have used the leather glove, but also a welder's helmet and a suit of armour.

Eyes still watering as if I was distraught because the bird was leaving, and having almost literally lost my face, there was no way I could get that bird ready for those girls unless they wanted him cremated. Lip or not, I'm sure I could have managed that (just a match to his tail feathers and puff). Then I could have presented his ashes to them in a peanut butter jar with a big sign on it, saying, "There, put that in your pipe and smoke it."

As it was, I conquered the urge to make bird butter out of him by taking him to the living room section and putting him under my rocking chair, and then rocking back and forth, back and forth, eight or nine times.

Bird and I soon staggered in to see the first aid nurse, like we'd both gotten off a four-day binge at the local tavern. My speech was impaired. I had to pantomime my story. It took some time before she could understand what the trouble was.

"Did you bump into a wall and knock your teeth out? And why do you have such a grip on that bird," she said. Shaking the ferocious fiend in her face and pointing back to my lip with the same fist that held the bird, I came pretty close to taking a swing at the nurse as Finch face made another savage lunge with his beak and almost got my remaining lip. If this kept up, I'd soon be sinking onto the floor, a sobbing heap of bird bait. The bird should have been hanged, then tarred and defeathered.

After this re-enactment, the nurse got the message and laughing (laughing, mind you), gave me what appeared to be a lip transplant, two band-aids running horizontally across my mortally wounded lip. But I was a bit put out that the nurse didn't do something to teach that bird a lesson, like slapping him, spanking him, or giving him a damn good whipping. But what did she do? Instead of putting masking tape around his bill forever, and then sticking pins in him as anyone with good sense would have done, she talked baby talk to him, as if he had gotten his beak torn off, instead of me getting mine torn off. The nurse should have been spanked.

And to top it all off, do you know those two pretty (but stupid) girls went right ahead and bought old Finch the Ripper without even giving him a good pinch, and took him home to a nice, cosy cage, knowing full well he should have been put before a firing squad. The least they could have done was to sprinkle the bottom of his cage with tacks and ground glass. I wouldn't have gone near that bird again with a ten-foot leather glove and a machine gun.

I had just gotten rid of the girls and the flippant finch when an elderly woman came into the store and said she wanted a finch, too. Everybody was finch crazy.

The store also had a restaurant in it; the boss warned me that if the finches ever got out, heaven forbid, to try and swish them away from the cafeteria area. It wouldn't be good business to have those ill-mannered finches hanging out there at lunchtime, flapping into customer's pancakes, picking off their noses, and smoking cigars.

Anyway, this lady pointed to a cage that held five finches. She was quite adamant about the one she wanted (bless her heart). They all looked alike to me— hideous— but she wanted the one on the far left. So I reached in and just at that moment one of the savage creatures flew right at my eyes. Taken by surprise, I leaned too hard on the cage. It fell with a smash to the floor, and all five birds flapped out, laughing up a storm. After making three or four sweeps around the full length of the store like a flock of migrating geese, they made their resting perch about thirty-five feet over the sandwich counter at noon hour.

Grabbing for the net, I was off on my hunt again, like a rare butterfly collector. One of the waitresses pointed to a stepladder that was in the back kitchen. What went on next was a great circus performance for the dining customers. Time and time again I'd make a swipe toward the birds with the net, going "shoo, shoo." Even on top of the stepladder, those birds were still twenty feet above me, and every few seconds there was a white souvenir deposited on the cutting table as the cooking staff tried to capture it in midair.

Those five innocent birds were a fine feathered sight to see, all sitting in a straight line like they were on a hydro wire, preening their feathers, unconcerned, sometimes looking down at the fools below them. I was getting nowhere with the net, so I took off my suit coat, preparing for battle, and aimed for the five sit-ups, except that the coat took a different route and almost smothered an elderly man who was just getting ready to reach for another spoonful of soup.

"Oh Lord, Oh Lord, I'm blind," were the muffled words I could hear from the old man as he fell off his stool and onto the floor, shrouded in my jacket. I rushed back down the stepladder to revive the old fellow, who was more in shock than he was hurt. When he found out what had happened, he laughed and laughed, saying, "Just help me up." He was in even better spirits when he saw the waitress bringing him another bowl of soup on the house, with one of the finch's calling cards missing the soup by a hair.

The old fellow thought of a remedy to get the five finches out of the cafeteria. He suggested we hook up a garden hose to the taps in the washroom, which we did. It only took one squirt and the whole five flapped toward the front entrance. But it was a good ten days before we got that flock of finches herded back to the cages, and that was mainly by starving them.

I managed to grab one for the elderly lady. I don't think it was the one she wanted, but at that point I didn't care if it was an albatross. She was going to take what she got. The store had learned a good lesson through all this. We learned never to put more than one finch in a cage, unless there was someone in the store we had it in for. And when someone wanted to buy a finch, the cage automatically went with the bird, whether the buyer wanted it or not. They could keep their children in it if they wanted to.

The bird door was never opened by us, and we talked confidently and happily to the buyer, warning them to be careful when they opened the door of the cage at home, but never quite telling them that all hell could break loose and even strong nations might fall.

The only thing that makes me happy now when I think of those long-beaked, black, feathery not-a-bit-friendly finches is the knowledge that they are behind bars for life, with no chance for parole. I've often wondered if any of their buyers have had to be fitted for artificial lips and fingers.

20

Eddy

It was March, 1950, and I was working in Portsmouth, Virginia. My brother-in-law, Eddy, had just arrived from working in the oil fields in Texas. He was blond, blue-eyed, good-looking and about fifteen years my junior. Many times he'd introduce me to members of the opposite sex as his father. He was as full of the devil as I was, and we were always having fun with each other.

Eddy and I were both trying to save money, so we'd always try to get the cheapest groceries possible. In Virginia on Sunday mornings you could buy chicken wings, livers, gizzards and hearts for about twelve cents a pound. That was our kind of price. We'd get there at ten a.m. sharp and take all forty packages of the chicken parts. Rather embarrassed while paying for them, we'd say, "Well, this will hold the cats for a while," leaving the clerks to believe we had about one hundred and thirty cats. And inside a week, Ed and I would be back for more— for our cats.

One day we were there for only a few groceries. I got Ed to push the cart, and reminded him not to spend too much because our rent was due. Of course, we didn't forgot our 'cat food'. We cleaned up on the gizzards and hearts again, which came to four or five dollars. Then we got milk, bread, butter and a few cans of this and that. Then I asked Ed to go way down the other end of the store to get some paprika. While he was gone, I put twelve cans of frozen lobster in the cart and hid them way down under our regular fare.

Then Ed returned with the paprika and pushed the cart up to the cash register to unload. I peeked at him from another aisle to catch his reaction. Our normal bill would have been quite high at $12.00, but this time the clerk said $38.00, which would be equivalent to $120.00 today. Ed first came close to tears, and then to fainting. With a sick grin and too embarrassed to tell her he didn't have that kind of money, especially with six people waiting in line behind him, he said, "The other man is paying for it."

"Well, go get him and make it fast," the clerk said, as Eddy ran to find me, telling me hurriedly, "The chicken gizzards must have gone up. Everything came to $38.00."

He and I rushed over as I told the woman innocently, "There must be something wrong with the cash register." Then she said, "It's the lobster that put the amount up." Both of us said in astonished unison, "Lobsters???" Ed said, "We must have the wrong basket." I said, "The lobster isn't ours. But we'll take all those chicken wings, livers and hearts (our cat food)." It wasn't until we were on our way home that Ed looked me in the eye and said, "It was you who put the lobster in the basket. I thought they were cans of soup."

It was the middle of April and Ed and I would be travelling back to New Brunswick in a few weeks. Getting set to leave warm Virginia, I usually tried to get a couple of days tan so I'd look like I'd been living in the South for the past six months. But we were working every day and had no time to lay in the sun.

That afternoon I was in a drugstore, searching for shampoo and toothpaste, when I found a bottle of something called Man Tan on a shelf with all kinds of suntan lotion. Reading a bit on the side of the bottle, it said it was an overnight miracle, and you didn't have to lie in the sun for a minute. It said you just rubbed it on you at night and you would be a brown beauty by morning.

It was fairly expensive, but Ed and I each bought a quart. I was never one to read directions in great detail. Never had time. Just the big lettering was all I went by. 'Tan overnight' was all I cared for. We'd be gorgeous when we got home. Artists would probably ask to sculpt us.

The Man Tan was the same consistency as rubbing alcohol. Back at our apartment at nine p.m., Ed and I rubbed ourselves with the liquid. We used an entire bottle between us, mainly on our faces, necks, and arms to the elbows. We applied every drop and it didn't do one thing for us. We were as white as snow. We might as well have rubbed pure water on us.

As we were falling asleep, I kept saying to Eddy, "How can they charge that kind of money for a bunch of lies? I'm taking that other bottle back first thing in the morning and giving them a piece of my mind."

After a good night's sleep, I was the first to awaken next morning. I sat up, rubbed my eyes, and looked lazily around. Then I saw my arms. I looked like I was wearing a khaki shirt, and hollered in amazement, "Ed, are you awake?" Ed mumbled something and then sat up. We looked at each other and screeched. Having gone to sleep as poor white trash, something drastic had taken place during the night. I looked like Al Jolson waking up next to a blond, blue-eyed Uncle Remus, both of us with bad cases of orangish, yellowish, brownish jaundice.

Ed looked like he had been dipped in a vat of iodine. Jumping out of bed, I rushed to the mirror. I looked like a reincarnation of Ghandi, only I was striped. "My God, what's the matter with us?" Ed suggested we might have hepatitis from eating all the chicken livers.

I said, "I don't feel sick." At this time, we were both half-scared to death, but killing ourselves laughing. Then I saw the Man Tan bottle. Grabbing it, I went over the directions very thoroughly. There it was in black and white telling us to use a small quantity, not to go overboard, and to apply it uniformly and carefully by rubbing it gently and evenly. If we had used it properly, there should have been enough in that quart to last the two of us for three months. My head looked like a striped, yellowish-brown basketball. The directions also warned to wash your hands immediately after use to get it off your palms. My palms looked like I had smoked two hundred packages of cigarettes a day for one hundred and fifty years.

We both rushed to the sink and slapped the soap and water to us, but it didn't change a pore. We scrubbed and scrubbed with warm, soapy water. Still nothing changed. I said to Ed, "I'm not moving out the door today. I'm phoning in sick." Eddy had been doing some odd painting jobs around Portsmouth since he came from Texas, so he called his boss and said he couldn't make it to his job. Later that evening, he and I, looking like cat burglars, sneaked down the back way to the drugstore to return the second bottle.

Looking like we should have been singing a duet of "Swanee," I asked the girl why she didn't tell us about the stuff. She said, "You're supposed to rub just a little bit on. You fellows look like you bathed in it." Then she burst out laughing along with us.

We laughed all that night. But the following day, I told Ed, "I'll have to go to work." So I concocted a new face by rubbing Noxzema and powder quite thickly over my entire Man-Tanned face and neck. When my boss saw me sitting behind my desk, he turned white as popcorn and asked me seriously if I was sick. He said, "You look like a corpse." I said, "I didn't eat breakfast." He looked at me again and said, "I think it must be your liver kicking up." So I went along with him and took off another day with his consent.

Ed was still at the apartment when I got home, and he said he had washed his face and neck a hundred times, with no change whatsoever. It just wouldn't come off.

Soon after this, we packed our bags and headed for Canada, a couple of make-believe Southerners with a tan that took two solid months just to fade before anyone could find out what race we belonged to. Each time Ed and I went into a drugstore after that, one of us would pipe up and say, "Do you sell Man Tan?"

21

Who Done It?

The small factory that I worked for in Boston had at its height about twenty men working there. Sometimes kids would come in after school and work a few hours for minimum wage. Some of them would bark about the wages, then quit and go someplace else.

Henry, a good buddy of mine from Amherst, N.S., had helped me get my job. He had worked there for three years, so he was able to show me the ropes when I first went to work.

The factory was a two-story job, with all the large machines downstairs, while upstairs the majority of the people worked, going to the lower level when required to use a machine.

There was one new, very well-kept men's toilet upstairs, to be used only by the two main bosses, Johnny and Ned. Every other male worker knew their toilet was downstairs. It had been there from the time the factory first opened, and by the looks of it, maybe even before. It reminded me of a map, with blue, square, round and oval veins all through it.

Work started at eight a.m. Living close to Henry, he always picked me up and we usually arrived at seven-thirty a.m., always the first workers on the scene. On the way to work this day, Henry said, as we neared the factory, "You know, Andy boy, I'll have to go right to the toilet when we get there, if I can make it." Having just had a breakfast of prunes, he had taken the words right out of my mouth. In fact, I felt I needed to go worse than him, but I didn't utter a word.

Henry parked the car and unlocked the building. "Andy, there's no one here for half an hour. I'm going to use the bosses' john," he said. "Okay," I said, taking a chance just answering him.

I staggered down the ten steps to the old john which looked tired and worn and was missing the seat. We were taught never to sit on a strange seat, especially when it wasn't there, because it harboured every incurable disease ever invented. I could have suspended myself over the toilet with my feet standing on the floor, but that would have put an awful strain on the calves of my legs. So I did what I used to do in our outhouses in wintertime. I stood up on the toilet, balancing myself neatly over the ancient appliance. Just beginning to set my mind on my job, I heard a noise like an earthquake as the whole toilet crumbled beneath my feet. There wasn't a four-inch piece of john left in the watery pile of rubble. My breathing stopped and, I believe, my heart, and luckily production halted from the sheer shock of the predicament. I was not able to continue.

My partner upstairs was used to covering the toilet for half an hour, so I left him alone and didn't say one word about what had happened to anyone— too embarrassing. I didn't tell Henry for the main reason that he'd be the first one the bosses would ask, and he wouldn't have to lie for me. The water was still flowing from what looked like an artesian well, and small pieces of crockery were rolling along with the flow like pebbles in a flash flood. It was a sickening sight to look at with the day just beginning, and I with my mission not even completed.

Starting up the stairs very cautiously, I went to my desk and waited for the other men and the bosses to arrive. Henry was just buttoning up and walking towards me, saying how much better he felt. Now the workers were coming in and getting into position at their benches. Next came the bosses. Still no one had gone downstairs. Henry, as was his habit every morning, switched on the light from upstairs to shine light down below. Taking odd peeks now and then while everyone was engaged in their work, I figured that at the speed that flow of water was racing towards the stairs, it would soon be upstairs with us.

It wasn't until an hour later that a young worker strode by whistling, with a steel rack in his hand, heading for downstairs. He was only seconds descending when I'm sure I was the first to hear his yell, "My God, Johnny, come see the water. What happened?" The whole crew made a mad dash for the stairs, me in the rear, playing it really safe.

The bosses tried desperately to stop the water. Henry said, "No one was down here this morning," saying it so honestly and surely that I almost believed it myself.

"Well," said one of the bosses, "you fellows get back to your benches. I'm calling the police." In a matter of minutes, a police car pulled up and three uniformed policemen came striding in to solve the mystery that Houdini would have missed.

Anything spoken down below could be heard upstairs if you were listening hard, and I was. One policeman said to the boss, "Did you have any trouble with school kids when they were working here?"

"Well," said Johnny, "a few wanted a big raise after working a few hours, so I fired them." Chest out, chin in and an arrogant face, one of the policemen said, "That's your trouble." And with that, he pointed to a window that had been raised two inches to let out the foul air.

Looking back at the crumbled toilet, one fellow said, "That john was smashed with a heavy instrument. You can tell, because it's in so many small pieces." All three detectives came upstairs to get a little more information about the school kids, ordering Johnny to put locks on the downstairs windows where the culprits must have gotten in. They also said that it wasn't a one-man job. All my motors stopped at the toilet's sudden demise, I was thinking, but if it had held my weight a few more seconds, it would have been a one-man job.

Lighting up cigarettes and signing a few papers, they gave us important looks as if to say, "Call us anytime. Nobody's ever fooled us yet," never dreaming the crusher was on the same floor as them.

Six hours more work, everyone had lots of time to think up reasons for the crumbled toilet. I suggested gas could have accumulated in the pipes and when the pressure built up, the pipes had no alternative but to explode (as I was ready to do at that moment), blowing the john to niblets.

Arriving home, met by my wife and daughter, I told them I wouldn't eat for an hour; I took my paper and sat leisurely on our john, which held me real good. I browsed through to see if I could find any police news about the "Flogging of the John" with a blunt instrument, and thinking, "It's a shame what school kids get away with today."

22

Johnny, My Love

At one time I worked for a small factory just outside Boston where rubber handles for pliers and other tools were made. It was a great place to work. One Christmas Eve at noon, one of the bosses, Johnny, said, "Everything stops. We're having a party." Of course, I didn't try to talk him out of it.

It was the custom of our bosses to send bottles of V.O. to their customers, and they had ten cases left over, so the drinks were plentiful. An afternoon of anything goes was enjoyed; I remember I even step-danced for the bunch.

Hours later, as all the employees were shaking hands and going off to their respective homes, I was feeling much lighter on my feet than when I had come to work. It was only a few blocks to my apartment, and luckily I had walked to work. This gave me a good excuse to drink that extra one for the road.

Three blocks to home was nothing. My temperature was soaring high and scorching the snowflakes as they fell on me. I didn't have to worry how my feet were working. I did a waltz clog all the way home.

But I had to pass a delicatessen which was run by an Italian woman. Every morning and evening to and from work, I passed this store and I saw the same sign in the window: 'Fresh Herrings for Sale'. In school, we were always taught that the plural of herring was herring; we had eaten enough herring in our day to know what two was called. The sign used to get on my nerves and I used to say, "Some day I'm going to go in and tell her the difference."

This was the day. Stumbling in, I babbled on and on to her about taking the 's' off the word 'herrings'. But after the argument, she in Italian and me in Gaelic, I became the loser. She threw a wet cake at me and almost stopped my breathing.

Home I shuffled, dripping cake. Rhoda met me at the door and was a bit surprised. I wanted my wife to know it wasn't my fault, so I blurted out, "They had their Christmas party," leaving her to believe they had forced me to imbibe and had then thrown cake batter at me.

Rhoda wasn't too worried. She just said, "Andy, Johnny sent us a lovely Christmas card today." (Johnny was the big boss.) After I had removed my coat, Rhoda said, "We have no more cards left. It's four p.m., so you'd better go to the store before they close." It was snowing quite heavy, but my pores were still giving off heat. I struck out for the store, and it wasn't until I was a half a block away from home that I realized I had no coat on.

Only half an hour before closing time I found a clerk in the store and told her I wanted a big, expensive card for Johnny. "Sorry," she said, "we only have what you see here," which was almost a naked rack. But I did see one I took a liking to, so I took it and had to get the clerk to find an envelope for it. It all took time, but I managed my mission. Now I had to mail it right away so it would have a December 24th postmark on it. I stamped it and mailed it. My deed was done.

I turned to leave the store, but walked headlong into a two-way mirror. It threw me back about five feet and I landed in a ball position with my arms wrapped around my face. Three men and a woman unrolled me and looked at my head, which was starting to look a bit like a pumpkin. Someone gave me a drink of water, which I didn't need, and told me to breathe deeply for a few minutes. I thought they were going to take my picture.

At last I found my way home. Christmas came on Sunday that year. Early Monday morning, the boys at work razzed me all day. They kept asking me if I was looking for a raise, or if I was going into partnership with Johnny. Later I found out why. There on Johnny's desk was a great big birthday card, not even a Christmas card, with large bold letters, saying:

TO MY DARLING SWEETHEART, Andy.

About a week after our Christmas party, I entered a drugstore about a block from my apartment looking for some razor blades. I picked them up and was getting in the lineup for the cash register when the clerk, with a line of about ten or twelve people ahead of me, rushed out from behind the register and said, "Harry, where have you been for so long?" There were tears of joy and adoration in his eyes. He looked at me like someone would look if their brother had been held as a prisoner in China for twenty years and he had just unexpectedly come across him while shopping. I had never seen the man before in my life.

I was in a rush to get home for supper, so I didn't have the time or the heart to explain to him that I couldn't remember him from any place. Instead, I went along with him. This was the worse thing I could have done. He looked at me seriously and said, "Are you at the same job?" What could I say but "Yes"? He said, "I left after they hired those two hippies. But you're still there? My, my."

Meanwhile, the customers were still held up and wondering why the clerk was mesmerized at the sight of me. Finally, I was able to get away from him after telling him I'd recovered fully from 'that operation', and that my sister had not married 'that evil beast'.

After I told the fellows at work, they said, "Andy, we'll go to the store with you tonight and see his response for ourselves." Three buddies followed me into the drugstore at a distance, during a busy part of the evening. Just like the night before, the guy hollered, "Harry, Harry!" and left more bewildered customers to run to my side, saying, "It's so good to see you," shaking my hands and hugging me, and to hell with the lineup of customers.

I could see my buddies behind a partition in a fit of laughter, not letting him see them. It got so I was embarrassed to go to the drugstore. For a while I had to quit smoking and shaving, suffer headaches, and I smelled bad.

But when I started to go back in again, I'd sneak in, but he usually spied me, and even if he was right in the middle of making change for a five-hundred-dollar bill, he'd leave everything— open till, wide-eyed, disgruntled customers— and holler, "Harry." And there he'd come again, arm over my neck, saying, "Harry, I just can't believe it's you," and me saying under my breath, "I can't either." One of the last times I went in, he flew over to see me, saying, "Remember the day we hid the old fellow's jacket." Of course, I had to go along with him. I had dug my hole too deep to back out now. So I said, "Yes, did he ever find it?"; and he said, "You led him right to it, in the fridge."

I found out that the man wasn't insane; but if he wasn't, then I must have been. And I always had to be prepared for new questions and disgusted glares from his lineup of customers.

Many times when I went to pay for whatever I bought, he'd say, "This is on the house, Harry. I'll never forget the way you treated me in Bolivia." Now as far as Bolivia was concerned, I did walk in Bolivia one day, over a map that my daughter had laid out on the floor.

Anyway, whatever I did to help that druggist in Bolivia, I don't begrudge it one bit. And someday, when I get a little more money ahead, I may go to a lawyer and have my name changed to 'Harry'. Then I'll feel free to visit his drugstore at any time for my necessities with my head held high, and I won't feel like an imposter.

Still employed at the small factory on the outskirts of Boston, I was put on the bull gang with nine other men. We did all the loading and unloading, and we fixed up any parts of the building that needed repair.

This day we were pushing wheelbarrows full of cement. It was a job none of the fellows liked, but it had to be done. I was the skinniest of the lot. One of our bosses, a Polish fellow, must have taken pity on me, watching my spindly legs buckle in and out when I was in harness pushing the heavy cement, because he called me aside and put me on a much lighter job. He told me to water down all the barrows after the men were finished with them so the cement wouldn't harden in them.

So I just stood around holding a huge hose about three inches in circumference, and hosed down each wheelbarrow as it finished its work. Nearly finished ridding the last wheelbarrow of its cement, it was almost time to punch the clock.

I knew the water would be ice cold, so I decided I would take a good swig of it out of the hose. It came out with such a force I had to take little bites out of it from the side. I was really slurping it back, satisfying my thirst, when the boss came by and saw me drinking from the hose. "Oh, my lord, Andy," he said, "that water's polluted. It's coming directly from the Charles River." At that statement, I believe I coughed up a couple of fish.

He hollered, "Come with me," as he raced up the long stairway to the second floor, with me flying along behind him. Maybe he was going to pump my stomach by reversing the vacuum cleaner. He took me to the water fountain and told me to drink all I could. But when you're filled to the ears, how much can you drink? He kept telling me in broken English, "Dere's chlorine in it. Keep drinking it." It was starting to drip out my ears.

Then he dragged me to the first aid room and they tried to get me to drink more. At last I refused. Couldn't drink one more sup if they had pointed a gun at me. Next, they called the doctor and got orders from him for me to have a couple of quick whiskys on my way home from work. He said it would kill any germs.

Well, there are not many people who have as good an excuse as that to get sloshed. And I thought I just might be able to find a vacancy in my water-filled body for a few slugs. A buddy who accompanied me wished he had the same disease I had so he'd have an excuse to give his wife, since every drink I took, he followed suit.

After the first two quick ones, I can't say what it did for my body, but I felt I was able to fight with bare knuckles any sickness that befell me.

Rhoda thought I was working late. I didn't have a chance to phone her. Everyone at work had scared me to death before I entered the pub. After six or seven quickies, in case the first two were duds, my buddy and I carried each other out into the fresh air. As we were walking along the Charles River to our homes, he seemed to have a harder time walking than I did, and every so often he'd stop, point to the river, and say, "There's the cause of all our trouble." We came to his house first, and it was only fair that I go in with him to explain why we were two hours late and drunk to boot. Telling his wife the story, I blamed it all on the river, even had her husband drinking the same polluted water as me.

As I left, his wife was gently patting him on the back like she was trying to burp a baby, and she looked contented indeed that the doctor had given us the order to get drunk. A few more blocks to go and I was soon telling Rhoda the sad tale of how close I came to getting typhoid fever, arthritis, ingrown toenails, pimples, and a dozen other diseases if it hadn't been for the doctor's prescription. If not for that, Jim and I could have died in each other's arms. I could see a tear in Rhoda's eye as she commenced to fix me a bite to eat and, you know, I was beginning to get thirsty again.

23

Please Everybody, Sing "O Holy Night"

It was April, and Ed and I were getting ready for our bus trip home from Virginia. Days before, I had bought a lot of clothes for my wife and daughter and packed them in beside my own things. Jeans were very popular at this time, so I bought my mother-in-law, who was quite heavy, a very large pair, size 48. They were on sale for only two dollars and were so big they took up a small suitcase all by themselves.

Before Eddy went to work in Texas, he had been living in Massachusetts and was unemployed. While there he kept getting a bill for twelve dollars, some kind of tax. When he left for the oil fields, he hadn't paid it.

After a few months in Texas, he got a letter saying they wanted their money or they would travel to Texas to get it from him, even though we figured it out and it would have cost them about two hundred dollars to come and get twelve dollars. Anyway, Ed didn't pay any attention and it all blew over after a while.

The government that year had issued new identification cards (green cards), and when we boarded the bus in Virginia, from there to Boston, we must have been stopped ten times by the F.B.I. checking everybody's I.D. cards for something, we knew not what.

We didn't know who they were looking for, but I kept insisting to Ed they were after him for that twelve dollars. Meanwhile, Eddy was dressed pretty flashily, with a fancy blue suit and bow tie, and a number of people on the bus thought he was a rock-and-roll star. So when one F.B.I. asked him what he did for a living, Ed, always full of the devil, told him with a straight face he was a singer, and left it at that.

The bus stopped for three or four hours in Boston, so Eddy and I grabbed a bite to eat at a lunch counter. Now Eddy had a way of sitting with his arms held in such a position in front of his chest that from behind it looked a bit strange. We were sipping our tea when a lady who knew Eddy came up behind him, saying quite loudly and in alarm, "Great God, Ed. I didn't know you'd lost your arm." Ed felt a little foolish in front of the whole cafeteria and his fans from the bus, probably the first one-armed rock-and-roll singer they had ever met.

Recovering from this shock, Ed and I sauntered across a bridge overlooking the Charles River. We were sitting on a bench and looking at the water when out of the blue another detective came over to us and asked for our identification cards for the eleventh time that day. Glancing over both of ours, he kept looking at Eddy and then back at his card and then over at Eddy again.

Calling his buddy over from across the street, he said, "Have you ever seen those eyes before. I'm sure I've seen those eyes somewhere." Eddy's eyes widened, and while the detective was talking it over with his buddy, I whispered to Eddy, "They must know you're from Texas. Must be that twelve dollars they're after. And you do have those unmistakable piercing, beady blue eyes."

Eddy's little pig eyes got larger and larger and he swallowed many times. Finally, one detective said to the other, "No, I've never seen those identification cards. You must be wrong." All the time Eddy and I thought they were talking about recognizing his eyes. Instead, they were calling the I.D. cards, I's.

"Whew, that was a close call," said Eddy, as we walked back to the bus terminal and boarded the bus for Canada. When we landed in Bangor it was one p.m. and they told us the bus wouldn't be going on to New Brunswick until six p.m. that night because they had to fix something.

Not wanting to waste five hours sitting in Bangor, Ed and I said, "Let's take the train from here." So grabbing our luggage, we hailed a cab and off to the station we went, hoping there were no more F.B.I. agents after us.

At the train station, we checked to see when the next train was going. It wasn't leaving until the next morning, so I got on the phone to the bus terminal to find out they weren't going to wait to fix the bus, and that everybody going to Canada was leaving in a few minutes on another bus. Just our luck. Hollering into the phone, "Wait for us. Wait for us. We'll be right back," we grabbed a cab and made it back just before they left. But then, to complicate the matter even further, and to rile the bus passengers a little more, the cab driver couldn't find my small suitcase with my mother-in-law's jeans.

Well, what a hold-up that was, with everyone on the bus grinding their teeth, wanting to be on the road again. I kept telling the people on the bus that all my belongings were in it because they might have strung me up had they known the only thing in it was a pair of two dollar jeans for my mother-in-law which would fit the bus on which they were driving.

It was a father and son who drove the same cab, and the son had gone parking somewhere with his girlfriend with my suitcase in the trunk. The father had to track him down which must have taken two hours or more.

I went through hell for those jeans and so did everyone else on the bus. (As it was, when I got home, they were even too big for my mother-in-law, but she wore them fishing every day anyway, with a piece of clothesline tied around her waist.)

At last we were on our way home aboard a very disgruntled bus half-full of people. When Ed and I boarded in Bangor, we sat midway back where there were plenty of empty seats. Everyone else was sitting up front to get the heat better. As I was placing my little satchel under my seat, I looked down the aisle toward the back of the bus, and under the very last seat at the back I spied something that looked like a small bar of gold. Probably some Inca had misplaced it. It couldn't have belonged to anybody up front, because everybody there was too far away from the square nugget. I was going to get that mystery object when everyone got off if I had to do a headstand at the back of the bus.

Crossing the border at St. Stephen, New Brunswick, our bus driver was told to pull over into a special parking space; all the passengers were asked to take their belongings into the border crossing station for a thorough check.

When everyone else had gotten off the bus to go into the Immigration office, I slunk my way to the back of the bus, and after a few maneuvers of reaching and kicking with my feet, soon had the prize. But I didn't have a second to examine it because an officer called in through the open door to bring my suitcases into the building for checking. I crammed the unknown object deep into my coat pocket.

Eddy was just ahead of me at the end of the long line of people who were now inside the building opening up their valises, suitcases and purses, showing everything they had accumulated during their stay in the U.S., even eczema. Some of the officers scrutinizing everyone's belongings were quite saucy and strict.

I began thinking, "Wouldn't it be something if someone told one of the officers that she had a valuable nugget of gold when she got on the bus and someone must have taken it, because she couldn't find it anywhere." This thought was really wrestling with my mind. I reached down deep into my pocket, still not knowing what the thing was that I had found. I hadn't had time to look it over before the border crossing guard called me in. With my hand still engulfed in my coat pocket, I fingered it from end to end and top to bottom. I had no idea what it was, except it had to be a gold bar, probably from Fort Knox.

There were four people in front of Eddy and me before it was our turn to be searched. Still digging around at the gold brick in my pocket, I felt something that seemed to be a small wheel on the rich object. Secretly, I flicked it. With no warning, my pocket broke in a Christmas carol. I had Guy Lombardo's orchestra in my pocket. My pocket was tinkling out "O Holy Night." I nudged Eddy, who was just a few feet ahead of me, and whispered to him, "Get a load of this." Eddy at first couldn't tell where the sounds were coming from, and thought I had turned into a ventriloquist and was throwing my voice. Somehow, without attracting any attention but making a terrible grimace, I got him to understand it was coming from my pocket. I put my finger to my lips to make him be quiet about it. He just kept looking at my pocket, wondering what was going on and probably thinking I was as good a ventriloquist as Edgar Bergen if I could throw my voice and make a sound like that come out of my pocket.

I still didn't know what it was, nor what I should do to shut it up. I squeezed the gold thing as hard as I could with my hand, hoping to strangle the members of Guy's band. Then

I gripped my pocket until the blood went out of my fingers and my knuckles turned white, hoping to smother it and block the song.

I was just waiting for someone to hear it like I could and to then speak up and say, "There it is, that's my gold bar." Still trying to suffocate the song, I began whistling to give everyone the impression that the lilting melody was coming from me. Elbowing Eddy again, I encouraged him with my eyes to also begin whistling to cover where the song was coming from.

Frantically, inside my pocket I felt every portion of the thing. One lady asked me quietly if I could hear a Christmas song somewhere. I coughed quite loudly and satisfied her by saying, "It's coming from another room."

I never dreamed there was so much song to "O Holy Night." I was thinking, "Oh Holy Smokes, will it ever come to an end?" I was nearing the officer's counter when I urged Eddy to break into song. So the two of us were now going through the checkpoint counter with an officer digging through our underwear and socks, blasting out our rendition of "O Holy Night"; and it was Easter.

I then thought it best if we switched to humming really loudly, because as we now were right on top of the officer, our loud singing was starting to get on his nerves.

Noisily, Ed and I poured some more of our belongings out for the inspector, all the while humming away like a swarm of locust. I clanked and banged things more than I normally would have and smiled broadly as the other people shuffled around making all kinds of sounds. Oh, how I loved noises now.

Receiving an 'Okay' after the officer's search, I looked at him with pretended pain and said, "Is there a washroom around here?"

"Right down the hall to your left." Ed and I walked off together, singing "O Holy Night" again at the top of our lungs in time with my instrument.

We entered the toilet. Once inside one of the little stalls, I jammed my hand hard into my pocket and came up with the little object that wouldn't stop. It was a golden cigarette lighter with a music control in it. On closer inspection, I could tell it had been wound very tightly so that when I messed with it, I set it off. Explaining to Ed what had just transpired, I soon placed it in my suitcase and muffled it with many sets of underwear.

And now when I hear those musical gadgets playing, I think about what a night I put in many years ago, trying to gag a beautiful song with everyone watching Ed and me belt out "O Holy Night." On that spring night with green grass all around and tulips coming up, accompanied by an invisible instrument, everybody must have thought, "Now there's a couple of men with the Christmas spirit."

24

Santa Is a Mean Old Man

> Santa is a mean old man,
> Santa is a dandy,
> When I climbed his fire truck,
> He hated poor old Andy.

In December of 1975, shortly before my first book *Bread and Molasses* was published, my editor advised me to promote it as much as possible. So when a friend suggested the Springhill Santa Claus Parade, I went along with the idea, since Springhill was a mining town and I was the son of a miner.

As the creator of Andy's Dummy Farm, I find it hard to refer to any of my books without a few of my dummies in the picture. So early next morning, like cosmeticians, my wife and I began brightening up a few of my dummy characters before the parade was to start. Then I spied my kilt. This would be a great opportunity to show off my knobby knees and skinny physique to those people who had been waiting with bated breath.

Decked out in my kilt, I strapped three dandy dummies over the cab of my small camper truck, while one large one poked his head out of the back of the camper. I enlisted the help of my ten-year-old grandson, David, whose job it was to hide behind this dummy's huge frame and keep its limp arm waving furiously to spectators lining the streets, like the Queen.

A few quick signs with *Bread and Molasses* scribbled on them were wired to each side of the cab and we were ready to roll. We reached our destination just as the parade was lining up near Springhill's only hospital. (Little did I know I might soon need its services.) Rhoda took her position at the wheel. David lay in the back of the truck on three fat cushions, holding onto the big dummy whose face was peering out over the tailboard, which was down.

The temperature was about thirty degrees fahrenheit and cloudy. The wet, foggy day made me feel dull and humourless, especially with the fact that I wasn't used to cold knees and drafts around my posterior. With fifteen minutes to the start of the parade, I visited the liquor store to find something not too big, yet not too small, to help me on my cool walk.

Soon tightly clasped in my right hand was a half-pint of rum. But where was I to have my quick drop? With three minutes to parade time, I made for a corner of the big hospital and down the hatch went the Demerara, without a chaser. I didn't worry much about choking, as I figured I would save enough strength to stagger into the hospital and show them the empty bottle with hopes they'd understand the rest by the sound of my gagging. Luckily, it didn't come to that.

At first the toddy did nothing for me. I've taken cough medicine that affected me more. So back to the parade I rushed as fast as my kilt would swing, to find Rhoda about a block away, thinking I was plodding faithfully behind. Instead, I was almost in the next province.

In the distance, I could see a dummy's arm waving at me. At this point I came across one of the planners of the parade. I was feeling quite sorry for myself, since it looked like I was going to have to follow my truck for miles along the parade route. If I'd known this, I would have worn roller skates. I told the man my sad story, "I've come thirty-six miles to be in this parade (giving him the impression I had walked all the way), but it's so long, I'll freeze with this skirt on." I followed the man's eyes to my white, knobby knees as he said, "Why don't you get on board the fire engine?"

Feeling a little flushed by now (the stimulant was having its affect), I darted for the lovely, newly-purchased fire engine, the last vehicle in the parade. With the ease of a wildcat, I scrambled up to the top to find myself seated next to, of all people, Santa Claus. And I hadn't even made out my list yet.

Even though Santa Claus was masked, I could see by the twitching of his beard that he didn't like me being there one bit. When I told him one of the officials of the parade told me to ride on the fire engine, he looked me directly in the eye with his blue, twinkly ones and said, "No one is supposed to ride on this but the driver and me." Then his belly shook like a bowl full of jelly. I guess he felt that I was the competition and might be mistaken for Santa, with my beard and all, though a mite anorexic. If Santa had ever looked at me when I was five years old the way that guy did then, I would never have hung up my stocking again.

Santa and I were both up at the front of the huge truck, waving to the procession like fools, and to break the icy silence, I said, "Well, I'll go way back here to the end." In my condition, I felt I was at least half a mile from the old meanie, but after about ten minutes in this new location, seated atop many feet of icy hose (and me with a kilt on), I could tell by the way Santa Claus was gritting his teeth like a pit bull that he wished a real fire would start to see if I'd still stay aboard. I knew I'd be getting coal in my stocking this Christmas.

By this time, Rhoda was more than four blocks ahead of me, still thinking I was bouncing along behind her. I thought I could catch up with her somehow and continue on behind my little truck, where I'd be more at home. Besides, if I had stayed on the fire engine, I surely would have gotten into a fight with jolly old Saint Nick in front of all those kids.

So grasping my dummy in one arm and my cane (for dramatic effect) in the other (I'd been holding onto both since I got out of the truck), I slipped quietly off the fire engine without a glance at old Santa.

I realized I couldn't go barging into the other floats like someone who had gone berserk. They might think I was Paul Revere hollering to them, "The British are coming. The British are coming." The ordeal of catching my runaway truck was my mission. So running alongside the parade like one possessed, onlookers had only seconds to snap their pictures. Passing many floats before finding my own, people were amazed at the fleet-footed, bearded and skirted fool whizzing past them like a bat looking for some hair to land in.

Rhoda had been driving now for many minutes, thinking her loving husband was strutting behind her since the beginning of the parade. Instead, I had just gotten into step behind the truck. I was very warm, active and animated at this point, and I was really getting into the spirit of the thing.

My steps were high and I was proud to be a part of the parade, regardless of the fact that Santa might have been an escapee from the nearby prison.

I turned to the spectators, holding up the dummy I was carrying and waving my cane furiously, like an actor. Suddenly, the wind changed from a ten-mile-an-hour breeze to a thirty-mile-an-hour gale which, unknown to me, whipped up not only my kilt but the large pasteboard *Bread and Molasses* sign on the driver's side of our truck, cutting off the full view of the windshield to my wife. She braked abruptly while I was just inches from the truck, nodding to and fro at the spectators like a king during his coronation.

Now, while some people have fallen out of trucks before, very few, I am sure, have fallen into one. SMASHO, I flew across the lowered tailboard of the truck as though I had been shot from a cannon. I landed in a heap between David and a shocked dummy. My knees, which had just been starting to warm up, were now bruised and battered from my collision with the tailboard. Eventually I managed to untangle myself from the mess of David, the dummy, the pillows and the tailboard, to find Rhoda was again advancing at a snail's pace after a helpful female hand grabbed the sign and yanked it from its moorings.

Although I was close to crippled now in both legs, I showed no pain. It must have been the raw toddy sprouting up now and then that enabled me to fool the public. I jumped back from the truck like a circus performer, as if what had just gone on was merely a stunt planned to make the people laugh.

Limping with a devil-may-care stride along the parade route, I thanked heaven that both legs had been damaged and not just one, as the off-balance gait would have made me look conspicuous.

It's always good to be able to blame someone for predicaments like this. I wouldn't think of blaming myself. Why, I needed that toddy to keep me warm. And it wasn't Rhoda's fault the sign blew up and blocked her view. I'll bet you all know whose fault it was that I mangled my knees...it was Santa's fault.

Afterthought:

I'm still not sure, but I believe there may have been two fire engines in the parade, the one with Santa on it and the one on which the firemen were riding. This may have been the one I was supposed to hop aboard, but my eyes focused only on the shiny, new fire engine that held that right jolly old elf, whose white whiskers twitched at me so disgustedly.

25

A Tooth, a Tooth,
My Kingdom For a Tooth

I have never hesitated about having my picture taken, whether at the scene of an accident, while I'm brushing my teeth, in the midst of a mafia shootout, awakened at three a.m. for the sole purpose of saying 'Cheese', or just relaxing reading the *Reader's Digest* while seated on the toilet.

Managing a fake smile for each occasion, most of my pictures turned out rather well, if I do say so myself (and who else will?), except for two large front teeth like Bugs Bunny, one of which was the thickness of a dime shorter than the other. A good, open smile was all I needed to show off my Tiny Tim tooth. If I laughed on a slant, sliding my lips to the side like a horse eating a thistle, my disfigured tooth couldn't be noticed. But I couldn't spend my life eating thistles. Then again, with all the talk about fibre, all that roughage might have been good for me. You can't get much rougher roughage than a thistle.

But back to my teeth. The two teeth were firm and healthy, except for this discrepancy. Now please don't get the idea that I had only two. I also had a perfect set around them. One evening while scanning pictures of myself, I was wondering if I'd have to go through life with one short tooth and one long one, kind of like with a donkey's tooth and a dog's, side by side. One remedy would have been to refuse to have my picture taken, or never smile again, like the song. But not me, for whether broke, sad or moulting, there was nothing like the click of a camera for me to break into a homemade smile. I just couldn't keep my mouth shut. My jaws got lame from all the grinning, and I was beginning to look like Alfred E. Newman on *Mad* magazine.

I decided to visit the dentist, who would make me look like Clark Gable. I already had his ears. Knowing how many years it took to get an appointment, I told him I'd only be in town a week, giving him the impression I was on the run from the law. So I ended up with an appointment in three days, and began practising my smile for my new look when I wouldn't be sporting Long John Silver's legs in my mouth.

At last the day came. Sitting back in the big chair, I thought it would only be about a fifteen minute job, where he might even serve me a five-course meal at the same time. Because surely all he had to do was melt down some gold and pat it on the short tooth, like lengthening a popsicle stick with plastic wood. But no! I might have known he'd never use my recipe. Too easy.

Instead, from behind him he sneaked a big needle and, if I'm not mistaken (it's all a blur now), after tying my hands and feet so I couldn't put up a fuss, he loaded my gums with shot after shot of novocaine while he laughed and told jokes to his nurse. I felt he must have given me those extra shots because my mouth was so large, probably caused from all the grinning I'd been doing.

After I had convinced him I couldn't say anything with a 'W' or 'S' in it and, in fact, might never talk again, he started drilling like he was working on a cement sidewalk. But I didn't much care if he drilled the nerve right out of my face, because in a few minutes I'd be the proud smiler of identically-sized teeth and would be able to say, "Neahhh, what's up Doc?" proudly and without embarrassment, while crunching on my carrot.

Well, the fun began. First of all, he pulled my lip back so that it completely covered my left nostril. Then at one point, to get a good crack at me with his drill, he had my chair adjusted back so far that I was tipped completely upside down, doing a headstand. Good thing I knew Yoga. For two hours he drilled away at me all the way up to my nose. He then picked and picked and picked at my tooth, until I tried to bite his finger off. But then, to get even with me, he had his nurse spray water all over my head, ears and upper body until it cascaded down my back. Next, to show me who was really the boss, his evil accomplice, the nurse, working with a reverse vacuum cleaner, blew air at me until gravel, most of the debris in his office and, I believe, some dirt from the street flew into my eyes and mouth.

It was obvious the man was out to kill me, or to wear me down so much that I couldn't strike back once I saw the damage he had inflicted upon my helpless tooth. So two hours and twenty minutes later, after gliding his drill and a couple of motor boats to every portion of my mouth, and even under my arms, when he knew he really had me at his mercy, he said, "There now," and passed me a mirror, saying, "take a look." Bursting with anticipation to see the new me, I had been expecting a gold fringe all around the bottom of the short tooth to put it in line with my other one. But when I looked at my teeth in the mirror, all I could think of was that he must have handed me a trick mirror like they used in carnivals, because as I widened my smile like a Jack-O-Lantern, there appeared in the mirror a man with perfect teeth. Except right in the middle of my mouth a tiny yellow-eyed bean had taken up residence where the short tooth used to live.

I don't know what prevented me from screeching and tossing the mirror at him. After all I'd been through! I *would* be fortunate enough to get Dr. Jekyll for my dentist, I was thinking, as I babbled, "What happened? Where's the rest of my tooth?" I expected him to tell me that he got the drill going and just couldn't get it stopped in time, and that I should consider myself lucky to have both my cheeks intact.

Then he said, "You know, a crown fits over that stump." Now I knew I was princely looking, but a crown on that tooth would have been like putting a silk purse over a sow's ear. But he went on, "Once we get that capped, it will be even nicer looking than the tooth." The real question was, "Could it look any worse?" Only if he filed all my teeth right down to the gums. I couldn't see how he was ever going to remedy this mistake, even if he fitted me with a crown for my head.

Then I figured he should know what he's doing, he's the doctor. But why hadn't he told me of this drastic procedure beforehand, to ward off my coronary or his homicide, or at least asked my advice on how to do it. My method might have been a little more expensive, like a trip to some gold fields in the Yukon, but I wouldn't be walking around with a stump in my mouth and looking as if I should be flinging my cape over my shoulder, saying, "Good evening" and biting people on the neck with my yellow-eyed bean.

Why, when I entered his office I had everything in the world to be happy about. Now, in a few short hours, there was nothing left in life to smile about, unless the dentist who had de-toothed me fainted right in front of me. Then I could have taken one of his little hammers and knocked out most of his teeth.

I am happy to report, though, that I was able to get back at him to some extent, and it wasn't even intentional. I was living in Virginia at that time, where I worked with my brother, computing different individual's income tax. At the same time I visited the dentist, the U.S. government was cracking down on dentists and doctors, checking into their income; almost every day the I.R.S. had a new name on the news. So when I filled out a sheet for the dentist asking my occupation, I put tax man, which I had been for over twenty years. When I passed him the sheet, his face dropped and turned white. He went into the back of the office, then returned and told me the sum it cost to fix my tooth. The amount was minuscule compared to what I had been led to believe it would cost for such an involved procedure. But as any good Scotsman would do, I instantly paid him in full, before he came out of his trance.

Though he capped my stump, I can't say I really owned the cap. While I admit it looked nice and white on my peg tooth, nine-tenths of the time it wasn't there. It was in my dinner, working its way into the core of an apple like a worm, or in the very bottom of an ice cream cone, waiting patiently to be flossed. And, of course, sneezing was off limits since not only would I lose it, but there was a good chance I might wound someone with it, and chip off one of their ears. Flying out in the face of a good 'kerchoo', my cap was faster than a speeding bullet, more powerful than a locomotive, and able to leap tall buildings at a single bound. People around me would be shouting, "Look up in the sky, it's a bird, it's a plane. Nah, it's Andy's tooth, again." So I've learned to sneeze through my ear.

Throughout my life we moved around a lot, and each time I had trouble with my tooth I had to call on a different dentist in a different town to glue it back on. Dentists from Sydney to

Vancouver and from Maine to Florida had my cap in their hands one time or another. It is the same one I had thirty years ago, though it's now stooped and haggard with age. It's smaller, too, from wear, and it doesn't have that milky white look it used to. It reminds me of a midget's dirty toenail.

Each dentist would charge heavily because of the expression on my face saying, "Please, dentist, I look like the toothless old hag in *Macbeth*. I can't face the public like this." To some I even hinted at leaving them everything I had when I died, which might have happened right there in their office if they didn't glue my cap back on in a hurry.

During one harvest-time, I made three trips in one month to stick my crown on. After one good bite of corn, it took ages to identify my cap from the niblets. I hated to tell the dentist to put on plenty of glue, because it gave me the same feeling as when I was young and told a disgruntled clerk to put lots of chocolate on my sundae.

After one dental visit in which I paid the sum of twenty-five dollars just to have the cap stuck back on, I asked the money-mad fiend if I could buy some of this glue myself. He gave me a sarcastic grin as though I was secretly planning on making bombs to destroy the world.

One day, eating an apple while strolling through a tall field of grain proved to lead to one of the heaviest toothhunts in history. I didn't miss the tooth until I had eaten three-quarters of the apple. That touchy little peg had to have a cap on it before the next day, since I'd heard the neighbour was going to cut his grain. With night coming on, I got down like a dog smelling tracks and searched in vain. Maybe I could coax my neighbour to cut his grain the following day, or perhaps sell me that small parcel of land— to raise crowns on. I shouldn't have cut through his grain field in the first place. He could have had me hanged. And toothless, at that.

Home I ran for a flashlight, then back to the grain again. With a small tea strainer, I sifted through the mud as I kneed my way along. After about two hours in a straight line on my own tracks, the beam struck what looked like a small shell. I snatched at it as though catching a miller. Knowing the neighbour had spotted me in his grain with a light, I slipped the cap over my peg, marched up to his house and told him I had been picking dew worms. I didn't tell him I was now wearing one of them on my tooth.

I really could not get along without my cap. It was embarrassing when meeting people who spoke to me and expected an answer. It would have been all right if I had had a mouthful of crackers. That way, I could just spray them with crackers while I spoke. They wouldn't be able to see my vacancy and would think that my funny speech was the result of talking through crackers. But since crackers weren't always handy, why hadn't the good Lord given people the power to speak out of an ear in emergencies, as I had learned to sneeze through one. And then again, you hear of people who talk through their nose. I'll have to try that some time.

One time at a Christmas concert, I was picked to be the M.C. There was a small lunch before the seven p.m. start. On one tray were some fig bars and do I love them. It seemed no one else cared much for them, so I really lit into them. Digesting fig bars and waiting for the concert to begin, I could feel the fig seeds lodged between my teeth. I reached out and picked up a toothpick from a little bottleful they had on the table. Whatever jokes were told, I laughed heartily from the sidelines while at the same time reaching in with the toothpick and digging the seeds out of my teeth. I forgot about my invalid tooth and thought I was prodding around at a hardy tooth until, lo and behold, I catapulted my crown right onto the tray of leftover fig bars.

It happened so fast no one saw me, but I could feel the rush of air. I had to stand and introduce the next person, but I found it best to make my spiel never facing the crowd directly but with my head lowered, like I was very shy and praying. After I announced the next act, I asked the lady in charge if I could take a few of the fig cookies home to eat later, still with my head lowered like I was going to bunt someone. She said, "Help yourself, Andy." I could see my cap sort of standing up, leaning against one of the fig cookies. To make things look good, I began gathering up a few of the cookies until I had the chance to pounce on my cap like a cat on a mouse.

My next move was to tell the lady in charge that my hands were sticky after being such a greedbag over the cookies. So she waved me toward the toilet like I was a small toddler who'd dirtied his hands. Once there, like a long-time tobacco chewer,

I gnashed my teeth into a cake of Ivory soap as if I ate like this all the time. I worked the chunk of soap all round the stump of my tooth and then placed the cap neatly right over the soap. It held firmly, but out on the stage again I had to swallow the soap taste. It wouldn't have looked nice to start spitting and spitting on the stage unless I was doing an imitation of an old cowboy star, like Gabby Hayes.

My first sentence was a real tester for this soapy cap. "Theodore Shea will now recite for us 'We Three Kings of Orient Are'." I blurted it out successfully, then, as I went along through the whole evening, my cap held on and I only blew the occasional bubble into the audience, which soon burst from the heat of the lights.

My next really nerve-wracking experience with my cap came about thirteen years ago, before a T.V. interview to plug my first book, *Bread and Molasses*. The publishers took me out to dinner. I have no idea why I ordered steak. Had I realized the pressure it would put on my capped tooth, I would have ordered a bowl of froth with bursted bubbles.

I love eating with a bunch and enjoy every story each individual tells. But alas, as a rule, it is I who usually talks the most. As I was a Maritimer and my three friends were from Ontario, I was going on about the similarities between the two areas, like their water was just as wet as ours, and the fact that we both use flour to make bread. After chomping up a good bite of meat while telling them we have the same moon and sun as they do, only ours is a mite larger, my story was building to a climax when I felt that old familiar sensation of air coming through my tooth, like someone had pulled a cork out of me. My complexion changed. Conversation was instantly cut just as I was at the point of telling them 'Where the peck of pickled peppers was that Peter Piper picked.' My mouth was full of half-chewed food. I couldn't swallow it. But it wouldn't be proper to spit it all out on the table and then begin rummaging through it. Instead, like a cow, I kept chewing my cud, gently; then from time to time I would stop and tunnel vigorously through peas, turnips and potatoes with my sharply pointed tongue and a blob of meal, looking for the lost cap of the Incas. I finally found it because of many years experience and a talented tongue, and was able to force it back into position without using my hands. I should have been a magician. Look ma, no fingers. If only I had gotten that crazy dentist in Virginia to sharpen the end of my tongue so I could manipulate the cap onto the stump in these emergencies. As it was, I know my tongue, from all the years of probing and prodding to keep the cap on, had lengthened considerably. I should now have been able to catch flies really fast.

In the restaurant, I put my cap back on my stump in seconds, as though I was resting between paragraphs and politely allowing my listeners to get a few words in, to cream their coffee and to butter their rolls. I felt like asking one of them, "Do you have any crazy glue on you?" but didn't know what to tell him I wanted it for. I could have told them a friend of mine was making a model church out of toothpicks, and it really took a lot of glue. I cut my steak into splinters and washed it down with coffee without even chewing, like a seagull gulping back a fish. I then brought my talk to a fast end.

From the restaurant to the studio was the next move. I was quite confident. Too confident. My first ten minutes were great, until I began talking about this character who whistled while he talked. He was known as Ed the whistler, a deacon in our church. Whistling out sentences, my mouth began to dry and my upper lip caught up over my peg tooth. Then, just as the interviewer turned around to pick up my book to show the audience, I whistled out a word so excitedly that I blew my cap right onto his pant leg. I had two choices. I could stand up, look out at the cameras and say, "I just blew my cap onto the interviewer's lap and I have to get it now." But would they understand? I mean, how many people do you know who wear their cap in their mouth? Or I could have said, "I just blew my crown onto the M.C.'s pant leg." But the audience would have thought I was arrogantly displaying my royalty and would have lost all respect for me.

No, I would have to wait until the M.C. turned around again to put my book back. Then very softly I would pluck my cap from his pants as gently as a butterfly landing on a mushroom. I just hoped he wouldn't notice it shining up at him and brush it onto the floor where it would get stepped on. Then it would be to heck with cameras and interviews. I'd be on my hands and knees under his seat, probably with the camera coming in for a close-up on my rear. If that happened, I'd have to tell them I was a Moslem and Mecca was in that direction.

In the meantime, I was still imitating this whistling character back home, only it was no longer an act. I was the man. When I said, "That's true," I lisped. I sounded exactly like Sylvester Pussycat. With my hand cupped over the vacant side of my mouth like I was whispering a secret, I wasn't saying nearly as much as when I was all in one piece. I should have told him to forget all about my book; that I was mainly on his show to do impressions of Sylvester Pussycat and Elmer Fudd. In fact, I felt like telling the M.C. that he should talk for a while and tell us all about his life; then get him onto a simple subject like, 'Why are we here?'

Eventually, the chance came to get my cap off his pant leg. The interviewer turned to put the book back. The camera followed me as I plunged for my tooth. The M.C.'s questioning eyes met mine with a look that said, "We get all kinds of nuts on this program." I sat back in my chair tightly gripping my cap.

He had seen me at his cuff. Throwing my head back and laughing like a fool, I whistled and lisped my explanation of what had just transpired. I had this uncontrollable urge to preface my sentence with 'Suffering Succotash', but squashed it. Instead, I said, "I juth can't thand lint on peopleth clotheth." While he was taking in my last sentence, I turned my face swiftly to the wall like those impersonators do to get into a new character. While the camera got a good shot of my bald spot, I slipped the tooth into position, turned around a new man just crawling with teeth and gave the viewers my best Colgate smile.

Why couldn't that first dentist have put hinges on my cap or a tiny nut and bolt? It might have loosened for want of glue, but chances are slim that I'd lose it. But way back then I was so sure that I was to have a perfect tooth to take me into eternity that I would have laughed out loud right in his face and then bitten him if the dentist had asked me if I was willing to buy a fifty pound can of glue and two hundred extra caps. Now I have to go through life scared to chomp into a cone of soft ice cream.

What I would like to know is, what do those movie stars do who have all their teeth capped? What a sight they'd be if their caps all came off at once. They'd never work again. With all those tiny upside-down pyramids in their mouths, they'd be lucky to get to play the part of a wolf.

26

Come Back, Little Rhoda

A while back was one of the few times in forty-seven years that I became a bachelor. Rhoda was going on vacation. She had been preparing me for it two months in advance, and all I heard day after day was instructions.

"Andy, the black pot is in the wood stove oven. Don't put it on full heat or it will melt." Well, she didn't have to worry about that. I'd never use the black pot. It's too hard to clean. And I despise washing dishes. Don't want to even see a dirty glass lying around. If I can't find the time to wash it, I'll smash it against the wall like the Russians do and throw it in the garbage. (Tourists would come to see the dummies and if they got thirsty, I'd even have them drink water from a cupped hand, knowing they'd leave and take their dirty hands with them.) My aim was to have no dirty dishes if it meant giving them all away to the neighbours.

Years ago, my twin, Murray, found a way to get rid of dirty dishes; when I really felt I had to eat, I used his scheme. After a meal of peas, potatoes, turnip and codfish, he'd put some leftovers on each of the dirty plates and place them in the refrigerator. I also adopted the method of an old lady at home who used to say, "Why wash the frying pan today? We'll be using it tomorrow." What did it matter that my fridge was so full of plates that I'd soon have to eat my meals on a barn shingle.

Just before Rhoda left, she mopped up the tile in the kitchen, saying, "Try to keep it clean." So I gave up walking on it. I learned to fly around the kitchen and if I tired out some, I just hung on the light switch for a few minutes till I got my wind back.

Her next instruction was, "When you take a bath, don't leave a rim around the tub." So I quit bathing. Then she told me that the *Dutch* cleanser was in the cupboard under the sink, and I was to keep the toilet bowl clean. So I haven't used the toilet in three weeks. I will again one day, I hope, when Rhoda comes home. But I wouldn't dare get on the scales. When you don't eat, you lose weight. But then again, since all toilet privileges have been cut off, it may balance itself out.

I'll bet Rhoda will be some jealous, though, when I pick her up at the airport and deliver her to our doorstep, and she sees how I've learned to fly from the porch step right across the kitchen to perch on a small shelf, without even touching the floor she cleaned before she left.

The night before Rhoda left on her vacation, she said to me in a serious voice, "Don't tell anyone I'm gone away." She thought someone might come and take me. I wish someone had. But who would want me, not even bathed?

Her next order was, "At night, don't sit near a lighted window. Someone could shoot you," though when Rhoda was home there were many nights when I sat in front of a lighted window, and only got half-shot.

Then came, "Don't kill flies on the clean windows." Now, there are billions of flies in our house in the fall, so instead of squashing them all over the windows I just place a saucer of syrup on the floor for them. Then I simply slaughter the pests by coming down on all of them at once with a round-mouthed shovel.

She also told me, "When it rains, don't let the dog in unless you wipe her feet." Luckily, I was able to buy two tiny pair of rubber boots made for babies so that when she gets wet, she just discards each little boot out in the porch and pads barefoot across the kitchen, much the same as I do. That is, when I'm not flying.

Rhoda even turned into a weather forecaster before she left. She knew there would be a change in the weather while she was gone, and she was right. We've had frost the past few nights. But do I care? Not a bit. Because before she went away, Rhoda planked thirteen woollen blankets on our bed to keep me warm. It takes me some time to burrow under the clothes, and whatever position I start out in, I have to stay in for the rest of the night, no matter if I'm dying of itch. Next morning

I have to bore my way back up to the surface again, like a diver ascending from the depths of the ocean.

And no matter how neatly I try to make the bed, it looks stupid. We have only one side we can get out of and it's rough trying to get a blanket to set right against the wall. It doubles over with every throw I make and deepens the thickness of blankets at the back of the bed. I fling myself on the bed to straighten out the mess, then I find the blankets seem to have shrunk before my eyes. It may be because I have put them on sideways, but I really don't know how Rhoda does it.

I finally decided that when I woke up I had more to do than start making a bed. So each morning I just left it as it was and jumped right back into the same mess again that night. It did backfire, though, because the other night I dreamt I was in Iran and they were going to hang me. When I woke up, I had two sheets locked tightly around my neck. But by that time I didn't much care if they did hang me, because my lower parts were numb from being exposed to the cold house by the criss-crossed blankets.

There's something funny about the pillow, too, since Rhoda left. It's grown legs. When Rhoda was home, I used to be able to control the pillow. But here alone, it seems as soon as I close an eye for the night my pillow begins to crawl. I eventually find it next morning under the bed, down at the foot, on the floor, or out in the hallway.

During this vacation of Rhoda's, I had a silk shirt that I wore all the time. I loved the style and the way it fit me. I had been wearing it for two weeks so I decided to wash it, knowing Rhoda wouldn't be home for a while yet. I gave my silk favourite a good dousing and then added a pint of bleach. I allowed it to rest in the ocean of Javex for about four hours, as I'd seen Rhoda do. The sun was still shining, so I went to the basin to hang my shirt out to dry. At this point, I saw that it wouldn't take up too much room on the clothesline. All that was left of it was six buttons from the belly of the shirt, plus two others, which an autopsy would have revealed came off the sleeves.

As the days went by, I thought I would at least make an attempt to do things for myself. It had been days since I ate and it was lunchtime. So I decided to cook myself a steak. And this is what happened....

Without my glasses on, I'm a dud around electric stoves. OFF and HIGH look the same to me. I flapped my steak on and naturally turned on the wrong burner. At the same time, some tourists in a motor home were pulling into my yard. So out I loped to escort the people around the Dummy Farm. After about fifteen minutes of laughing and talking, I remembered my steak. But I couldn't say to them, "Just a minute till I go see my steak." They would think I was a surveyor or that I'd just killed Dracula.

I was in conversation with a woman, so it was 'Good Night, Irene'. She asked more questions than an immigration officer when you're trying to smuggle your mother-in-law across the border in the trunk. Finally, I cut her off in the middle of a question and shot for the house as if there was a nest of vipers in my pants.

I found my steak still red and almost walking around the kitchen. Two burners were crimson. One held a lone tea bag in a glass percolator. I reached for the pot of tea; the bottom dropped out of the percolator. On the second burner, a covered frying pan sizzled at full speed.

I then remembered I had started my breakfast earlier, but some other tourists had shown up and I had forgotten about it. My bacon and eggs had turned into an undernourished toad and two dilapidated alder twigs.

Then I closed off all buttons and satisfied myself by thinking, "At least I'll have a good cup of tea." So I plugged the toaster in for the tea kettle! Fifteen minutes later, the water was not even tepid, so I grabbed the kettle and swept out onto the lawn like Scarlet in *Gone With the Wind*. A batch of tourists were looking at the dummies. I beckoned for one of the men to come over. Then, shaking the kettle in his face, I almost blamed him for it not working. "And it's only three days old," I ranted at him. The man was from New Jersey and he accepted the blame pretty well after my raving. I guess New Jersey people are like that. It wasn't until later that night that I pulled out the toaster cord and plugged in my kettle, which in seconds began to purr away. I felt like calling New Jersey and telling the guy it wasn't his fault after all.

I have another problem when I'm left alone. Sometimes I fall asleep downstairs on the couch at dusk and I wake up in darkness. I have claustrophobia so I try not to get excited because I'd smother quickly. I don't holler, but I'm weak. I don't know what room I'm in; I don't recognize any part of the house. I just keep wandering around very cautiously, quietly knocking over plants and pictures and trying to remember where the light switch is. I know sometimes I walk for hours, leaving nothing behind me but a gentle path of destruction.

I try braille, feeling objects and trying to guess what they are. It seems that in the short sleep I have had on the couch, someone has not only rearranged the furniture, but has put strange new items all over the house to baffle me. After I had fallen asleep, a real cut-up sneaked into my house and placed a baby's plastic pool, a headdress from Tutankhamen's tomb, a small load of gravel, a beach ball, one-half a cord of wood and two pit bulls in very strategic areas.

On my last unlit tramp around my house, I found the phone. I would not let go of it for dear life, figuring if my breath kept getting shorter, I could tell the operator, "No, I'm not Jim Bakker making an obscene phone call. I'm Andy MacDonald, lost in the dark and I can't find my kitchen."

On my nocturnal meanderings, I acquire many bruises from the legs of rocking chairs and iron pots containing plants. On one of my hikes I was fortunate enough to run into the TV with such a whack that it snapped on. Then I could see to turn on the main light and survey my kingdom. The house looked as if a marauder had torn it apart looking for secret information we had stuffed inside our walls.

I tried to keep the floor fairly tidy while Rhoda was gone when I got too tired to fly. I swept every ten days whether it needed it or not. As the babes in the woods were found by their trail of crumbs, you could find me by my trail of leaves on my shoes— right up to the bed. First time in living memory our house was full of leaves. I'll have to have a bonfire in the house. By the way, I don't mop the floor at all, except for the day of Rhoda's return, whether she's been gone for two days or eleven years.

At the time of writing this paragraph, Rhoda is gone on another vacation and I haven't touched the bed she made two weeks ago. I now have one little blanket and a tired pillow, and we three just sleep. Then when I awake for the day, I have my little bunk looking neat in three and one-half seconds. I unpin my pillow from the neck of my pyjamas, then peek out the window to see if there are any tourists.

My underwear, shirts, hankies, towels and face cloths just keep piling up, but it's not much of a worry. I keep buying new ones.

I go downstairs to eat my bacon raw. I don't have patience to wait until it's cooked into black, tasteless strips. I never leave the kettle plugged in very long, so the poor little tea bag does not get scalded. It just gets flushed with warm water, which makes it difficult for steeping. But in one way it's an advantage. Now I don't have to struggle trying to hold onto a hot tea bag.

Next I call my wife's brother, Percy, from up the lane and ask him of he knows where Rhoda keeps the pepper and that little pan to boil eggs in.

Last, but not least, comes a prayer, "Please, Rhoda, don't leave me alone any more. Helpless, that's what I am, helpless."

27

Pick Them Up Without Bending

It was time for another of my wife's vacations. So having packed her bags and cleaned the house the night before, she was up first thing next morning for an early start. I carried her suitcases out to the car, and she and her sister were soon on their way to Toronto.

Now if someone had told Rhoda an hour after she left me that I had been seen out in my field not able to straighten up, she would have laughed in their face and then had them committed.

Back in the house, I was thinking that two weeks would go by quickly, so I'd see how much I could accomplish while Rhoda was gone. There were thousands of blackberries in my back field. So off I went to pick a few. It was early September and the night before we had a heavy frost, so the foot-high Timothy was still very wet.

I decided not to sit or kneel or I would be drenched; also people would think I was praying. The berries spread out before me like caviar. I stooped over to pick them and kept up that stance for over an hour, not allowing my pant legs to get wet. My pot was filling up fast and my cup runneth over, so I thought I'd mosey along toward the house to get another container. However, moseying was not in the cards for me, because as I made a move to straighten up, I discovered that every part of my body was locked solid. I had turned to stone. Well, it was better than a pillar of salt.

When I attempted to stand, I couldn't. I didn't change from the position I had been picking in. I just fell over onto my side in the wet grass in the shape of a U. I was a good half-mile from my house. No one knew I was in the back field picking berries except the dog, and she was right beside me.

If a plane had been searching for an oversized crab, they might have spotted me. But when they did, they'd have had to carry me home with a crane, whooping or not.

I could see Little Boy was becoming embarrassed at the way I was flaying around there like a bass someone had just landed, all crumpled up on the ground. I tried once again to get up, and in my lurch I upset all my berries, then lay in them, squashing every one and leaving a stain on the back of my shirt like I had been shot with a bazooka.

Well, I had to do something about heading for home, unless I decided to live out in the field grazing like a cow until Rhoda came home in two weeks. I tried my best to untie myself, but I seemed to be in the shape of a piece of clothing someone had wrung out. I found the only way to think of getting home was to crawl on all fours side by side with Little Boy, who thought I was playing with her. I rested at frequent intervals to gain some wind. This made Little Boy impatient and she barked for me to keep going. If I had had any extra strength left, I might have torn her fur out in patches.

After a half-hour, I arrived near my house still on all fours. I rocked my way up the step to unlock the door. This caused terrific pain and I fell in on the kitchen floor. By this time, Little Boy had become disgusted and tired of playing with me and thought the whole joke had gone on long enough. I just wished there was some way I could seek revenge against Little Boy so she could put her back out and have to walk on all fours.

At home now I felt much safer. I knew if I had to, I could nose my way to the phone and say, "Listen, doctor, I've tried everything, but I can't get off my knees. I'm planning on killing the dog. Get here pronto." But then he'd probably get the idea that I was a minister who mistreated animals and would only send me over some knee pads, along with some Greenpeace people hand in hand with the S.P.C.A.

I then recalled something my daughter had told me a few weeks ago, that if you had trouble with your back, just place a small golf ball under the sore spot and lie on it. I knew we had a golf ball somewhere in the house (from my days with Arnold Palmer). But now to find it. If anyone had come in at this point, they would have thought I was licking the carpet.

A good two hours had passed since I had walked out to my picking grounds. With my head level with the floor and my eyes peering in all directions, I spied the golf ball. Like a setting hen pulling her eggs under her with her beak, I used my beak to grab the golf ball, and in no time I was rolling along the floor like I was riding on a tricycle. Then I turned into a baby tornado. I upset bookcases and flower pots. Books were strewn all across the floor while I was speeding along out of control on one wheel, through the mud of the flower pots.

The ball didn't do much good at first because it kept getting lost in my loose, berry-stained shirt. Then it found the sore spot and soon, after rolling around heaven all day on my golf ball, I found I could sit up. It seemed as though it had been years since I had sat up, though by now it had just been about three hours. Like an infant just learning to walk, I felt proud.

With full use of my arms now, my aim was to stand. However, I figured I'd need a rope about eight feet long. So I golfballed my way to an old cupboard, skimming along like I was lying on a roller skate, and got some rope. Then I came back up to the sitting position. It was my aim now to ring the top corner of the electric stove and pull myself to a standing position, after which I would become a steeplejack and hot foot it to the top of the CN Tower.

Clearing all obstacles out of my way before applying a cow-catcher's knot in the rope, I flung my lasso at the stove and nabbed the third electric kettle I had bought in three months. It bounced and bounced and bounced on the floor in several pieces. "Well, now," was all I could say, knowing I was the only one who could hear.

I believe the shock of breaking my third kettle moved a few discs in my back, because I unscrewed my body and clambered to my feet in pain. This was the first time I had been standing on my own for hours. Waddling over to my cane rack like a baby with a full diaper, I captured two canes and, looking like a walrus on dry land, I lumbered along from flipper to flipper as I tried to learn to walk again.

It was all right if I kept an even walk, but if I miscalculated a step by one-quarter of an inch, my spinal column seemed to part as if disintegrating because I'd been zapped by a laser gun. I had just seconds to pick the spot where I was to drop, whether over a cliff or onto a busy railroad track, both of which I have in my house.

The pain in my back had also cut down on the volume of my speech, and who did I have to talk to anyway but the dog and my conscience. Every word I spoke aloud ended up in a coughing whisper, as if I were in a house filled with smoke and was slowly being asphyxiated.

Having too much pride to call a neighbour or a doctor, I, who had been a going concern a few hours ago, could now barely put one foot in front of the other. So I took three Tylenol and jacked myself up the stairs with my two canes, like a First World War veteran. A warm bed lulled me to sleep. Next morning, with a slight loss of memory during the night, I hopped out of bed like I was normal, which I haven't been since I was born, then doubled up and rolled along the floor like a bowling ball. I struck the wall full force without even getting a spare. I came to a halt about three inches from the top of the stairs.

As I write this, it's nearly forty-eight hours since the berry -picking mishap. I'm still badly misshapen and suffering and, do you know, I don't even have a berry to show for all my troubles. They're all over the ground in my back field. The only way I'd get a taste of blackberries is if I boiled my shirt and drank the juice. And it's going to be just too bad if a neighbour comes and says to me, "Andy, have you seen that lower field of yours? It's white with mushrooms." As far as I'm concerned, they can stay there until they decide to get up off their butts and walk into my house under their own steam.

I found out the hard way: as the back is bent, so grows the man. If I was to get into that four-legged position again, Rhoda would have to place me in a kennel when she got home.

28

My Drugs Were Legal

If you know me at all, you'll by now have realized that I'm always ready to play a trick or two. About six years ago— I hadn't been back to Cape Breton for quite a while— I began planning my pranks on the way down .

Arriving in Sydney Mines after a three-hundred-mile drive, daylight was nearing its end; just the right time for some fun with a neighbour I was brought up with. I drove my car to another good friend, Tommy, who ran a grocery store. Once there, I caught up on all the recent gossip about Nettie, my neighbour of many years ago. As luck would have it, Nettie's brother was in the store and more than willing to help me. He said his sister was visiting someone next door, but her husband, Les, was at home.

Now, I had known Les from birth. I believe he delivered me. He was always number one in my book, quiet and kind. You just didn't want to get his dander up. So, of course, this is what I planned to do. I got Nettie's brother to tell me everything that had happened to Nettie's husband, Les, in the past week. He said Les had been making payments on a stove from Simpson's each month, and he had decided to save paying the carrying charges by pinching every penny so he could pay it all off. And about a week ago, he had sent Simpson's a money order for the balance. I was storing and filing all these facts like a computer. The time had arrived for some deviltry.

I dialled Les's number. Changing my voice considerably, I asked Les very politely, using a high-pitched woman's voice, if this was the residence of Lester Alderson. "Yes, sir," came the reply; so I continued in my whiney voice, reminiscent of

Lilly Tomlin (one ringie dingie), "We haven't received any payment on your stove for a few months now, Mr. Alderson."

Knowing full well that he paid all his bills promptly, I heard a loud outburst on the other end, and saw a flare go off up in the sky. He sputtered, "I sent the final payment last week." To add more fuel to his fire, I said in my wheedling voice, "You'd be surprised how many of our customers give us that same sob story. Now, if you don't get your payment to us immediately, we'll have to come to your house and take the stove back." After this statement, I could feel the phone jiggle in my hands, and little puffs of smoke came out of the receiver.

Les was the kind to almost go without eating to pay off his debts, and was also the kind to go berserk if he was accused of not paying them. He was furious and his shivering, sputtering, stuttering, spitting voice changed. He began hollering so loud I had to move the phone inches from my ear. He said, "You just come round to the house. I'll be ready for you. Just you come ahead. I'll throw the stove right at you."

Egging him on even more, I said, "I'll bet you're a big man, eh?" The phone was burning my ear when he said, "You'll find out. Just come near the place and you'll see how big I am." There was not much more damage I could do after this, unless I sent the police to his house to seize his stove.

I hung up and that was the end of that trick, knowing I'd left Les on the verge of hysteria. By this time it was about ten p.m. and quite dark. Les only lived about a block from Tommy's grocery store, so I walked over to his house carrying a small briefcase. I didn't dare take my car because Les might have thought that I was the agent from Simpson's and thrown the stove at me.

Cautiously, I walked to the door and rapped softly, giving him the impression I was a small child. He yanked open the door, took one look at me and started laughing, "Andy, you S.O.B., it had to be you on the phone. You sent my blood pressure sky high." He continued laughing so hard he had to lie down on the couch. When he came back to his senses, after wiping the tears from his eyes, he said, "Let's get Nettie. She's next door." I guess he figured he put up with so much fooling from me that he would get revenge not on me, but on Nettie, his wife.

Now, to sham Nettie, I was to be an encyclopedia salesman. I phoned her at her friend's house, disguising my voice as I had with Les, only this time I spoke like a descrepit old man. It was about ten-thirty p.m. as I spoke to Nettie. "Hello, Mrs. Alderson. I'm over at your house with your husband. I'm selling encyclopedias and your husband seems quite interested in buying a set. But he'd like to get your consent before we clinch the deal." Surprisingly, she said, "Well, whatever he says is all right with me," as though they had plenty of money to throw around.

She was in the middle of a card game and this was disturbing her play. I continued on, "Well, I have to have the signatures of the two of you." Finally, Nettie asked the all important question, "How much does the set cost?" I said in my very best old man's voice, "They're six hundred dollars, with no money down." I heard a thump on the other end, some muffled sounds and a serious voice saying, "I'll be right over."

In my briefcase I had a very curly wig, black sunglasses and a set of Mortimer Snurd teeth for occasions like this that I knew I would run into. And as Rhoda, my wife, was constantly after me to take vitamins, I had three different letters— A, B, C— and Brewer's yeast pills all in this briefcase. Les and I worked fast getting my hair on, my teeth in and my glasses on. I had pulled my collar way up around my neck and my briefcase was sitting at my feet, full of oodles of vitamins and papers which had absolutely nothing to do with encyclopedias.

Les was lying on a cot about ten feet from me, doing a terrific job of holding back a laugh. The door flew open and in swept Nettie, a large woman, who wouldn't be scared to tackle two men. She walked toward Les, but first took a couple of quick peeks at me and mumbled under her breath, "Where's his car?" Meanwhile, I was keeping my head lowered and had my hands constantly fluttering around my face.

In my trembling hands I had about four sheets of paper, and you could tell Nettie was wondering if Les had signed anything. Then she walked by Les really fast, whispering, thinking I couldn't hear her, "It's an old man to be out this late. How did he get here?"

Les couldn't answer any of these questions since he was red as a beet from trying not to laugh. Nettie settled down about five feet from me and studied me, trying her best to find out something. Each time she looked in my direction, I was prepared. I kept swinging my hands across my face like I was in pain. I shuffled a few papers together, then said in a frail, squeaky, old man's voice, "It's a real good deal."

"But six hundred dollars is a lot of money," objected Nettie. At this, I made terrible grimaces, rubbed my face, hiccoughed and said, "But there's no down payment." Then I dug down deep into my briefcase and came up with four vitamin C. I threw them into my mouth and gobbled them up as though my life depended on them.

I dug into my vitamins at five minute intervals, all the time pretending I was trying to hide them from her, yet knowing she was watching every move I made. "Holy cripes," she said, quite loud, "It's even a dope fiend."

With that, I made a thousand faces, scratched my head, squinted my eyes up tightly and cleared my throat in a grisly way. I could hear her saying to Les, "It's lousy, too." Then to me she said, "I don't think we could make the payments. There's only one of us working." But I kept throwing back at her, "But there is *no* down payment," knowing she must have been thinking, "My God, with no down payment, what must the monthly payments be?" Each time I'd fling back a few more pills with my shaking hands, attack my head again, and make some more hideous faces while Nettie rolled her eyes to the ceiling. But there's only so much a frail old man can do without laughing out loud, and I had reached my limit.

I reached up, took off the glasses and the wig, and took out the teeth. "Well, Andy MacDonald, you son of a bitch," hollered Nettie, as Les fell right off the couch onto the floor laughing until he couldn't laugh any more. Nettie, in hysterics by then, got the same idea as Les, to play a trick on her next-door neighbour.

Before Nettie phoned her, I got all the dirt on her friend. Nettie said she had been trying to sell an old stove for months, and she finally couldn't even give it away. So she had gotten a couple of kids to lug it down to the cliffs and throw it over into the Atlantic a few days before.

On the phone, Nettie told Mabel that she and Les had bought the encyclopedias and that the salesman wanted to see her. Mabel tried to object, "Girl, it's too late." But Nettie wouldn't let her off the hook and told her the salesman said if she didn't come over, he was going to her house.

Meantime, I was rigging up again for a woman I had never met, getting into my disguise and setting out plenty of vitamins. (Don't worry about how many vitamin C pills you take in an hour. I took a whole bottle and I'm writing this.) Soon the door opened without a knock. Mabel walked in and sneaked a look at me just as Nettie had as she passed my slouched, shaking body.

Nettie had a towel in her hand, using it to wipe across her mouth to smother her laughs. Les had taken up his position on the lounge again, lying straight out and getting redder and redder all the time.

Mabel, not knowing the price of the set, asked Nettie, though she was still peering at my actions. I don't know how Nettie kept herself from bursting out laughing, but she said in a good, strong voice, and with authority, as if it was only a drop in the bucket, "They're only six hundred dollars."

"My God," said Mabel, "we have a set home now and we only paid two hundred dollars for them a year ago." I reached for my pills, giving her to believe it was people like her who had caused my drug addiction. I made many faces, scratched my wig, eyes, hands and back. Then I said, "But my set is two years newer," and then started on her with, "I need *no* down payment." That seemed to make her squirm more. Nettie was rubbing her mouth harder with the towel. Into the pills I rummaged again. I could hear Nettie say to Mabel, "Girl, it must have forty different pills it's been taking."

With my head lowered and my hands dancing around my head like I was shooing away blackflies, I downed the vitamins and said, "I also take old chairs, tables and lamps, and I give a good price on old stoves." At this I was interrupted by a smothered titter from Les, while Mabel said, "I knew I should have kept that damned stove another few days." Then Mabel continued, "My husband would kill me if I signed for another set of encyclopedias. Besides, I haven't cracked a book of the other set yet."

Mabel was all prepared to leave me now to eat my pills and scratch and grin, so I took off my disguise while Nettie told her who I was. The place was in an uproar for an hour. And Nettie told me next day that that night she had laughed and laughed all night long. And Les got so mad because he had to get up early next morning that he made Nettie take her pillow and sleep in the parlour on the settee.

So if anyone wants their marriage ruined, just give me a call, but let me know in advance so I can bring my vitamins. It seems I'm a very poor salesman without them.